PLACE NAMES OF AFRICA, 1935-1986:

A Political Gazetteer

by
EUGENE C. KIRCHHERR

The Scarecrow Press, Inc.
Metuchen, N.J., & London
1987

This is a completely revised, enlarged, and updated edition
of the author's earlier monographs, the last of which appeared
under the title, <u>Abyssinia to Zimbabwe: A Guide to the Political Units of Africa in the Period 1947-1978</u>, 3rd ed. (Papers in International Studies, Africa Series No. 25 [Athens,
Ohio: Ohio University Center of International Studies, 1979]).

Library of Congress Cataloging-in-Publication Data

Kirchherr, Eugene C.
    Place names of Africa, 1935-1986.

    Rev. enl., and updated ed. of: Abyssinia to
Zimbabwe.
    Bibliography: p.
    1. Africa--Politics and government--1945-1960.
2. Africa--Politics and government--1960-   .
3. Africa--Gazetteers. I. Kirchherr, Eugene C.
Abyssinia to Zimbabwe. II. Title.
DT31.K53 1987   911'.6   87-20765
ISBN 0-8108-2061-7

CONTENTS

ACKNOWLEDGMENTS

This updated and considerably enlarged political gazetteer of the principal African territories could not have been completed without the assistance of various individuals and organizations. I am grateful for the grants received from the Lucia Harrison Endowment Fund of the Department of Geography of Western Michigan University. That funding enabled me to pursue research at other libraries and to consult directly with appropriate officials or authorities. I am also indebted to the Department of Geography of Western Michigan University for making available typing and cartographic services during the preparation of this manuscript. The Department and the College of Arts and Sciences provided some released time from my teaching assignments during the winter semester of 1985, enabling me to pursue research on this project.

A number of new maps were drafted for this expanded version while several maps used in previous editions were revised or entirely redrawn. The formidable task of preparing almost two dozen maps was accomplished because I was fortunate to have the services of Ms. Mary Dillworth and Mr. Marc Freytag, two competent cartographers. Though neither is an Africanist, I could not have found more dedicated assistants. They gave painstaking attention to details in producing a number of maps designed especially for this book.

The gazetteer (Part Two) first entered a word processor through the skilled hands of Ms. Victoria Soboleski and Mrs. Celia Besbris. Typing the manuscript was one additional assignment for these already overburdened departmental secretaries. Cognizant of my deadlines, they attempted to work as often as time permitted on the manuscript. Subsequent to the

v

initial storage of the gazetteer in the word processor, they contributed many hours working with me on editing the manuscript, and I benefited from their helpful discernment of my typographical and syntactical lapses. Members of the staff of Waldo Library of Western Michigan University were, as always, generous in their assistance, sharing their expertise in the search for certain types of data and maps, and also in obtaining publications from other libraries.

I also wish to acknowledge the cooperation received from the Map Division of the Library of Congress, the U.S. Board on Geographic Names, the Office of the Geographer of the U.S. Department of State, and the Map Library of Michigan State University. Staff members of all those agencies graciously responded to my detailed inquiries on specific points with illuminating answers and materials.

I owe special thanks to numerous authorities known to me only through their published work. The thoroughly researched studies of many Africanists proved indispensable as sources in verifying historical, political, and geographical details. Regrettably, the selected bibliography (Part Four) does not identify all the individuals whose works were used. Indeed, had I attempted to list every book and article consulted, the result would have been a lengthy bibliographical sourcebook with little space for the gazetteer and supplementary notes.

I am truly indebted to those who in varied ways made immeasurable contributions to this undertaking. Nevertheless, I assume full responsibility for the overall organization of the book and also for the selection and interpretation of data presented in the text and maps. Believing that anyone consulting a gazetteer for basic information should not be given a potpourri of fact and opinion (with possibly heavy sprinklings of the latter), I have attempted to present the material in a concise, straightforward format and to maintain the highest possible accuracy in reporting dates and significant events.

Eugene C. Kirchherr
Professor of Geography
Western Michigan University
Kalamazoo, Michigan
December 1986

LIST OF MAPS

LIST OF TABLES

PART ONE: GENERAL INTRODUCTION

I.   THE NEED FOR A POLITICAL GAZETTEER

In the history of Africa, especially in the realm south
of the Sahara, the last quarter of the nineteenth century
was noteworthy as the period when European powers were
engaged in a competitive "scramble," each seeking to estab-
lish its authority over areas previously unclaimed and unde-
limited. Although spheres of influence would be contested
and boundaries realigned through the early part of the
twentieth century, by the end of the first World War, many
African political territories had assumed characteristic shapes
which in many cases remain recognizable even now. The
names of colonies and protectorates had also become fairly
standardized and would be retained for several decades.
Yet by the third quarter of the century, colonial powers
found they could not ignore demands for independence
voiced by a growing number of articulate, resolute African
leaders who were gaining a popular following. Through
the period of political transition, from the end of colonial
rule through the early post-independence years, new names
(toponyms) had begun to appear on the political map of
Africa.

Scholars have substantially documented the origin of
political organizations and nationalist movements in many African dependencies between World Wars I and II. Such evi-
dence of nationalist aspirations notwithstanding, in 1935, the
base year for this reference work, there were just four independent states on the continent: Egypt, Ethiopia, Liberia,
and the Union (now Republic) of South Africa (Fig. 1).
That condition remained unchanged until 1951 when Libya
became the first African state to achieve independence in the
post-World War II period.   Libya and other North African

states generally retained their familiar short-form names following independence, but did adopt long-form names for formal usage.

In sub-Saharan Africa, the former British colony of
the Gold Coast (including the Trust Territory of British
Togo) was first (1957) to be granted full independence;
"Ghana" was chosen as the name for the new nation.   Perhaps it was believed that new denominations would be similarly adopted by other states, signalizing the termination of
colonial rule.   Such a prediction was not entirely borne out
by subsequent developments, however.   The independent
status granted successively to various African states did not
in every instance result in the renaming of those states
(perhaps a concession to grateful map publishers).   Moreover, there would be occasions when the adoption of new
names clearly was attributable to reasons other than the
achievement of independence.

Even in the late 1940s, a general library collection of
Africana still could be shelved tidily in any available nook.
Some years later, the deluge of material on Africa began, at
a time when the political pattern was in a state of flux.
Students, teachers, and others began to discover inconsis-
tencies in the disparate names for major African states found
in atlases, books, and articles.   A new generation of students particularly was being challenged, often frustratingly
so, to master an incongruous mixture of obsolete colonial
names, other names adopted but used briefly, some new
names, and, of course, all the variants.   To compound the
confusion, some territories--the British Cameroons, for
example--seemingly had vanished from the map!

The first version of this gazetteer or geographical
dictionary of the names of the African territories was published in 1968.   The principal objective then was to fashion
a cross-indexed gazetteer, one designed for easy use in
tracing the different conventional names used for the major
African states.   The present gazetteer, substantially rewrit-
ten and expanded, still seeks to serve the same purpose, by
listing names used during all or part of five decades, from
January 1935 through December 1986.   As certain information
was not always appropriate for summarization within the text
of the gazetteer, a separate section of Supplementary Notes
was prepared (see Part Three).

As the emphasis is on primary political divisions of
Africa, economic and other forms of supranational associations are not generally mentioned in the gazetteer. In those
few instances where reference is made to such associations,
such as comments on the status of a number of dependencies
which were members of the French Community from 1958 to
1960, the relevance will be apparent.

II. PREPARATION OF THE GAZETTEER

Earlier editions of this political gazetteer covered the
periods 1951-1967, 1950-1974, and 1947-1978. The present
version considerably opens up the time frame, taking in just
over the half-century between 1935 and 1986. For the first
time, the period prior to World War II is included. The
choice of 1935 as the base year was not purely arbitrary.
Although it was not necessarily a pivotal year in modern
African history, it does represent a point in time by which
European powers appeared to have achieved total control, or
at least pacification, in most of their dependent territories.
(Even by the early 1930s when reporting of African affairs
tended to be exiguous, the colonial rulers in several territories were still being opposed by armed indigenous forces
unwilling to negotiate or sign treaties.) Admittedly, not all
international boundaries in Africa had been settled by 1935,
either, though a substantial number had been delimited;
boundary treaties and related issues were matters for dis-
cussion by representatives of the colonial powers, with African peoples largely absent in such proceedings. Finally, the
Italian invasion of Ethiopia in 1935 would open one of the
final chapters in Africa's colonial history.

Books, atlases, government reports, scholarly journals,
and general periodicals were perused to ascertain the usage
and variants of both former and present names--short-form
or common names as well as the official or long-form names--
applied to the major political divisions of Africa and nearby
islands during the past half-century. The investigation cen-
tered on usage in English-language publications, but details
were checked when necessary in French, Portuguese, and
Spanish sources. If several sources were found to be vague
or inconsistent on specific points, such problems were taken

up directly with embassies of African nations, the Office of
the Geographer in the U.S. Department of State, and the
U.S. Board on Geographic Names.

From notes of present and former names of each major
African state, a complete alphabetized listing of entries was
compiled. Primary entries consisted of the present name
(short- and long-form), with an explanation of principal
changes in the name and political status of the territory.
Former names are, for the most part, cross-referenced to
the primary entry. As the gazetteer is intended primarily
as a reference tool, the objective was to keep the entries
succinct, highlighting only pertinent changes from 1935
through 1986. Still, some length was unavoidable in writing
several entries; numerous or complex changes in the names
or status of several territories (e.g., NIGERIA and ZAIRE)
made it impossible to keep those entries brief.

The spelling of territorial names has not always been
either consistent or standardized. Names of such territories as LIBYA and FRENCH SUDAN were often printed as
LIBIA or SOUDAN, suggesting the writer or cartographer
opted to use a conventional foreign spelling. Even after a
territory is renamed, there occasionally may be an interim
of uncertainty concerning the proper spelling, or at least
an accepted English spelling if it differs from that of the
official language of the country. When the government of
Equatorial Guinea announced numerous toponymic changes
in 1973, the island of ANNOBON was renamed PAGALU,
though some sources were reporting the new name as PIG-
ALU. Again, when the government of UPPER VOLTA declared the country was being renamed in 1984, the new
name appeared with several variants, e.g., BOURKINA
FASSO, until the government finally issued a clarification
stating the correct name was BURKINA (although BURKINA
FASO was acceptable). Considering the scope and intent
of this gazetteer, it would not have been feasible to list
every known variation in spelling. Only if a particular
variant is determined to have been used over a period of
time is it included in the gazetteer.

III. NOTES ON THE MAPS

Each map was drawn specifically to meet anticipated
needs by users of the book. Possibly several additional
maps might have been drafted, but those provided at least
should spare one the nuisance of ferreting out special atlases or sheet maps. Users not familiar with the current
names and locations of the African nations are directed to
Figure 1, a serviceable political map of the continent.

The maps should enable the reader to better compre-
hend the nature of territorial realignments, boundary adjust-
ments, and similar modifications in political space. The
maps thus complement the text and are considered an integral
component of the book. Yet the inclusion of maps warrants
a word of caution with a disclaimer. Though drawn with
care, they should not be regarded as authoritative. Boundaries on a neatly produced map appear to be legally precise
lines acceptable to the governments involved. In reality the
boundaries shown are only highly generalized depictions on
relatively small-scale maps. Furthermore, the boundaries in
some areas are yet to be properly surveyed, and sections
along boundary courses may still be in dispute.

PART TWO: PLACE NAMES OF THE PRINCIPAL AFRICAN STATES AND ADJACENT ISLANDS

NOTES ON THE ORGANIZATION AND USE OF THE GAZETTEER

1. The alphabetized listing is based on the spelling of territorial names commonly used in books, articles, documents, and maps published in the English language. Variant forms of the names, because of their occasional use in English-language publications, are also included. The French spelling of territorial names, rather than the English spelling, was sometimes used for French colonies (e.g., TCHAD for CHAD). As French was retained as the official language in those states after becoming independent, French spellings can still be found for some countries in recent English-language publications.

2. Each primary entry for an African state includes both the current short-form or common name (e.g., TANZANIA) and the lengthier official title (e.g., UNITED REPUBLIC OF TANZANIA). The official or long-form names adopted by sovereign states are used in documents and official papers. In several countries, no long-form name has been adopted, or may not have been adopted at the time independence was attained. Many former English colonies and protectorates were formally proclaimed "Republics," though only some years after having achieved independence. Even when a long-form name has been changed substantially, the conventional short-form name may remain the same (refer to the entries for LIBYA and MADAGASCAR).

Current names (as of December 1986) are printed in

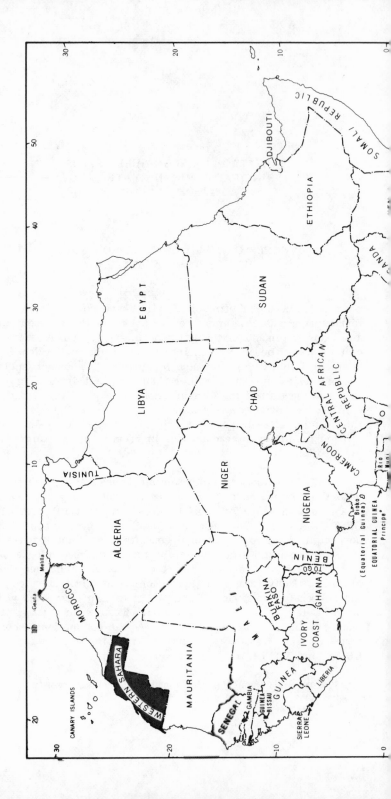

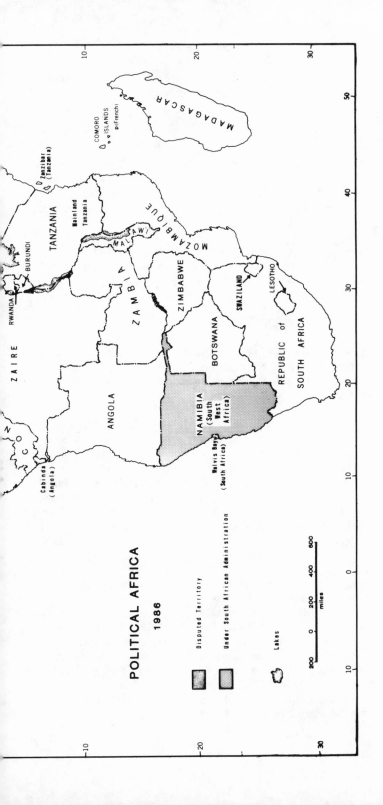

POLITICAL AFRICA

1986

Disputed Territory

Under South African Administration

Lakes

uppercase letters in the left column of the gazetteer
pages, e.g.,

NIGERIA or REPUBLIC
OF NIGERIA

In most cases, the primary entry for a specific country
is accompanied by a short review of changes in political
status and denomination during the period 1935-1986.
Explanatory "Notes and Comments" are printed in the
right column.

Former or obsolete names of the African political units
are also in uppercase letters, but indented and identified by a bullet mark.

•GOLD COAST
•SOUTHERN RHODESIA

Entries of this type are usually cross-referenced to the
current name. Nevertheless, where it was thought fit-
ting to note particular information on a former name (or
territory), a short commentary was added.

Names printed with only the first letters capitalized
(e.g., Cabinda) are used for special territories or names
such as the following: exclaves, islands, or internal
divisions (which can be mistakenly depicted or inter-
preted as being separate sovereign territories); currently used, though not necessarily official, alternate
names; and names not currently applied to a territory,
yet not strictly obsolete because they are still used for
other features or places (e.g., Cape Juby, Tanganyika).

3. In the explanatory "Notes and Comments" printed
in the right column, names listed elsewhere in the gazetteer
are printed in capitals when first cited, thereby serving as
cross-references. Current names are printed in regular capital letters (e.g., CENTRAL AFRICAN REPUBLIC), while
former or obsolete names are shown with a bullet mark
(•UBANGI-SHARI). The explicative material provides references to supplementary notes (abbreviated: Supp. Note)
found in Part Three. Also included are references to specific
maps. (A complete list of all the maps by number, title, and
page can be found with the front matter of the book.)

4. In the period covered by this reference work, several African political units were administered as mandated territories under the League of Nations (until 1946) and as Trust Territories under the United Nations (after 1946). An explanation of the special status and final disposition of those territories can be found in Supplementary Note I in Part Three.

•ABYSSINIA

Traditional name for the highland core region of ETHIOPIA. However, usage of ABYSSINIA persisted into the twentieth century as the alternate name for the modern Ethiopian state which evolved during the nineteenth century.

Comment: ABYSSINIA appears to have been used infrequently after World War II for by then ETHIOPIA was clearly recognized as the official name for the country.

•AEF

See •FRENCH EQUATORIAL AFRICA.

•AFAR(S) AND ISSA(S) TERRITORY

See DJIBOUTI.

African Party for the Independence of Guinea-Bissau and Cape Verde

See Supp. Note VI-D.

•AFRIQUE ÉQUATORIALE FRANÇAISE (AEF)

See •FRENCH EQUATORIAL AFRICA.

•AFRIQUE OCCIDENTALE FRANÇAISE (AOF)

See •FRENCH WEST AFRICA.

•AJUDÁ

See •SÃO JOÃO BAPTISTA DE AJUDÁ.

ALGERIA or DEMOCRATIC AND POPULAR REPUBLIC OF ALGERIA; also

Former French-administered territory in North Africa. Algeria consisted of two divisions under a centralized

PEOPLE'S DEMOCRATIC
REPUBLIC OF ALGERIA
(ALGÉRIE)

administration (Fig. 20). Northern
Algeria, divided into departments, was
in most respects governed as an integral part of metropolitan France. The
larger southern region was divided
into territories under military administration. Following the fall of France
in 1940, Algeria was controlled by the
collaborationist Vichy regime. In 1943,
the territory came under the control
of the Free French forces. The period
1954 to 1962 was marked by warfare
between Algerian revolutionary forces
and French troops. Algeria finally
achieved full independence on July 3,
1962; in September, the country was
proclaimed the DEMOCRATIC AND POP-
ULAR REPUBLIC OF ALGERIA.

Comments: 1. The Government-
General of Algeria had an exceptional
status among French dependencies. It
was not considered a "colony," nor
was it under the jurisdiction of the
French ministry responsible for colonial
territories.

2. From 1957 to 1962, the Southern
Territories were reorganized by French
decree into two •SAHARAN DEPART-
MENTS (Fig. 20). As so constituted,
the departments (also known as •FRENCH
SAHARA) collectively formed a separate
administrative entity. However, the
Saharan Departments were incorporated
into the independent Algerian state in
1962. (See Supp. Note IV-B.)

ALGÉRIE

See ALGERIA.

•ANGLO-EGYPTIAN
SUDAN

Former name for the REPUBLIC OF THE
SUDAN when it was administered jointly
by the British and Egyptian governments. The country achieved full independence in 1956.

ANGOLA or PEOPLE'S
REPUBLIC OF ANGOLA

Formerly a Portuguese overseas territory also known as •PORTUGUESE

WEST AFRICA; formally declared an Overseas Province in 1951, and designated an autonomous Portuguese state in 1972. ANGOLA, including the exclave of CABINDA, achieved independence on November 11, 1975.

Even as Portuguese withdrawal was underway in 1975, Angola was in the midst of a civil war involving three groups of nationalist forces. One group, the MPLA (English trans.: People's Movement for the Liberation of Angola) controlled the national capital of Luanda and the surrounding region; MPLA declared itself the legal government of the new PEOPLE'S REPUBLIC OF ANGOLA (also referred to as RPA, an abbreviation of the Portuguese name). MPLA (later becoming MPLA-PT) soon began receiving formal recognition from a number of governments.

Comment: In late 1975, two other anti-Portuguese movements (UNITA or National Union for the Independence of Angola, and FNLA or National Front for the Liberation of Angola) formed a short-lived coalition government known as the •DEMOCRATIC PEOPLE'S REPUBLIC OF ANGOLA. That coalition, opposed to MPLA, proved ineffective and was unsuccessful in obtaining either recognition or support as the legal government of the Angolan state. The coalition was inoperative by early 1976, but UNITA has since continued as an active insurgency movement, at times claiming control over extensive areas of southern and central Angola.

Annobón   Small island which is part of EQUATORIAL GUINEA (Fig. 5). From 1973 until the early 1980s, the island was known as •PAGALU.

•AOF   See •FRENCH WEST AFRICA.

Aozou (Aouzou) Strip   See CHAD and Fig. 13.

ARAB REPUBLIC OF   See EGYPT.
EGYPT

Archipel des Comores   See COMORO ISLANDS.

•AUTONOMOUS REPUB-   See TOGO.
LIC OF TOGO

Barotseland   British protectorate having special
                               status within the larger protectorate
                               of •NORTHERN RHODESIA (now
                               ZAMBIA). BAROTSELAND was ad-
                               ministered in the colonial period as
                               an integral unit of •NORTHERN
                               RHODESIA (Fig. 21).

                               Occasionally considered, even
                               through the early 1960s, were sug-
                               gestions to separate Barotseland from
                               •NORTHERN RHODESIA, and to desig-
                               nate it a separate overseas unit.
                               Nevertheless, when ZAMBIA became
                               independent in 1964, Barotseland was
                               fully incorporated into the national
                               territory.

                               Comment: The term Barotseland
                               is still used for the southwestern re-
                               gion of ZAMBIA.

•BASUTOLAND   See LESOTHO.

•BECHUANALAND   See BOTSWANA.
[PROTECTORATE]

•BELGIAN CONGO   See ZAIRE.

BENIN or PEOPLE's   Formerly known as DAHOMEY, one of
REPUBLIC OF BENIN   the territorial divisions of •FRENCH
(RÉPUBLIQUE POPULAIRE   WEST AFRICA (Fig. 19); was a colony
DU BÉNIN)   until 1946 and an Overseas Territory

from 1946 to 1958. Officially became
the •REPUBLIC OF DAHOMEY (RÉ-
PUBLIQUE DU DAHOMEY), an autonomous member state of the French Community, in December, 1958; the republic attained full independence on August 1, 1960. Dahomey annexed the
diminutive Portuguese enclave of •SÃO
JOÃO BAPTISTA DE AJUDÁ in 1961.
In December 1975, the country was
renamed PEOPLE'S REPUBLIC OF
BENIN. (See Supp. Note II-B.)

•BIAFRA or
REPUBLIC OF BIAFRA

Secessionist state established in May,
1967, when the former Eastern Region
proclaimed its independence from the
FEDERAL REPUBLIC OF NIGERIA
(Fig. 2). After the final surrender
of the Biafrans to federal forces in
January, 1970, the secessionist terri-
tory was again incorporated into the
Nigerian state. (See Supp. Note
VII-C.)

Bioko

Island long identified as FERNANDO
PO (or PÓO) which today forms one
of the two major divisions of the
state of EQUATORIAL GUINEA (along
with the mainland territory of RIO
MUNI). (See Fig. 5.)

The island underwent several name
changes between 1973 until the early
1980s, but is now officially BIOKO.
Nevertheless, Fernando Po is still
used as a variant name for the island. (See Supp. Note VI-B.)

BOPHUTHATSWANA or
REPUBLIC OF
BOPHUTHATSWANA

Formerly one of several "Black (or
tribal) Homelands" established within
the REPUBLIC OF SOUTH AFRICA
(Fig. 23). Granted full independence
by the South African government on
December 6, 1977. However, Bophuthatswana's sovereignty is recognized formally only by South Africa,
but by no other country, nor by the
United Nations. (See Supp. Note VIII.)

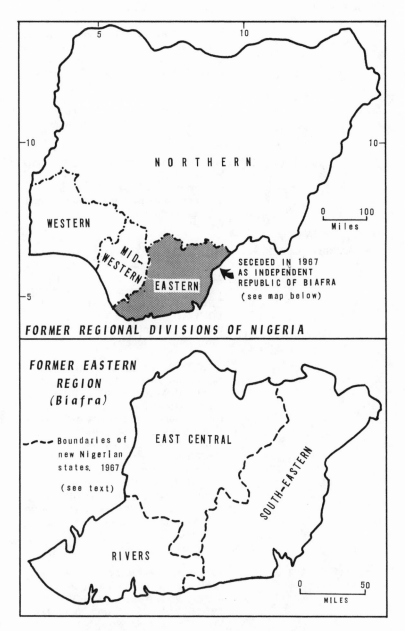

FORMER REGIONAL DIVISIONS OF NIGERIA

NORTHERN

WESTERN

MID-
WESTERN

EASTERN

SECEDED IN 1967
AS INDEPENDENT
REPUBLIC OF BIAFRA
(see map below)

0   100
Miles

FORMER EASTERN
REGION
(Biafra)

Boundaries of
new Nigerian
states. 1967

(see text)

EAST CENTRAL

SOUTH-EASTERN

RIVERS

0   50
MILES

Fig. 2.   Republic of Biafra, 1967-1970.

BOTSWANA or REPUBLIC
OF BOTSWANA

Formerly the British-administered
•BECHUANALAND PROTECTORATE,
and one of the three •HIGH COMMIS-
SION TERRITORIES of southern Africa
until 1964 (Fig. 22). Achieved full
independence as the REPUBLIC OF
BOTSWANA on September 30, 1966.
(See Supp. Note V-C.)

Comment. Until 1965, the administrative capital of the Bechuanaland
Protectorate was located in Mafeking,
SOUTH AFRICA (since renamed
Mafikeng and now part of BOPHUTHATS-
WANA). The territorial capital was
then relocated to Gaborone which subsequently became the national capital
of independent BOTSWANA.

•BRITISH CAMEROONS

Former British mandate (1922-1946)
and Trust Territory (1946-1961) (Fig.
17). As a U.N. Trust Territory, it
was formally designated •CAMEROONS
UNDER BRITISH (or UNITED KING-
DOM) ADMINISTRATION. The territory was administratively integrated
with British Nigeria.

BRITISH CAMEROONS consisted of
two parts, •NORTHERN [BRITISH]
CAMEROONS and •SOUTHERN [BRIT-
ISH] CAMEROONS (Fig. 3). Following
a U.N.-supervised plebiscite in Feb-
ruary 1961, the •SOUTHERN CAME-
ROONS joined with •REPUBLIC OF
CAMEROON (as then constituted) in
October to form the •FEDERAL RE-
PUBLIC OF CAMEROON (now again
simply REPUBLIC OF CAMEROON).
•NORTHERN CAMEROONS was annexed
into NIGERIA in June. (See Supp.
Note I-C.)

•BRITISH EAST AFRICA

Term used for the group of British-
administered territories in eastern
Africa, viz., •KENYA COLONY AND
PROTECTORATE, •UGANDA PROTEC-
TORATE, and •TANGANYIKA TERRI-
TORY (mandated area and, after 1946,

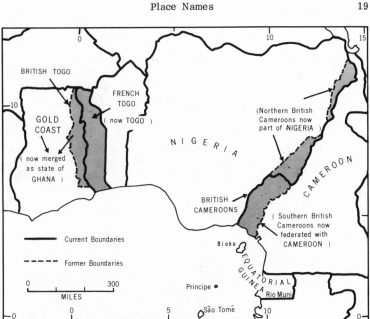

Fig. 3.   Mandates/Trust Territories of Togoland
and British Cameroons.

a U.N. Trust Territory); the offshore
protectorate of ZANZIBAR was also
often included in the group (Fig. 9).
All the territories eventually achieved
independence.

Comment: Although various services were organized on a regional
basis, the territories were never politically unified.

•BRITISH HIGH COM-   See •HIGH COMMISSION TERRITOR-
MISSION TERRITORIES   IES.

•BRITISH SOMALILAND   See •SOMALILAND PROTECTORATE.

•BRITISH SOUTH   Variant term for the •HIGH COMMIS-
AFRICAN TERRITORIES   SION TERRITORIES (q.v.) of southern Africa.

•BRITISH TOGO[LAND]   Former British-administered mandate
                             (under the League of Nations) until
                             1946, then a U.N. Trust Territory,
                             formally, the •TRUST TERRITORY OF
                             TOGOLAND UNDER BRITISH ADMIN-
                             ISTRATION. See Table 1 and
                             Fig. 3.

                             Trusteeship status terminated by
                             the U.N. in 1957, allowing the terri-
                             tory to be united with the British
                             •GOLD COAST to form the new inde-
                             pendent state of GHANA. (See Supp.
                             Note I-B.)

•BRITISH WEST AFRICA   Collective term applied in the colonial
                             period to the non-contiguous British
                             dependencies in West Africa, viz.,
                             GAMBIA, •GOLD COAST (now GHANA),
                             NIGERIA, and SIERRA LEONE. Each
                             of the territories was designated a
                             "Colony and Protectorate" ("Colony
                             and Protectorate of Gambia," for ex-
                             ample). The mandated areas (Trust
                             Territories after 1946) of •BRITISH
                             TOGO and •BRITISH CAMEROONS
                             also were often considered parts of
                             British West Africa (Fig. 3). "BRIT-
                             ISH WEST AFRICA" was primarily a
                             descriptive term. The British terri-
                             tories, each of which was governed
                             separately, were not politically uni-
                             fied or federated as were the colonies
                             of French West Africa.

BURKINA or   Formerly the French colony (later an
BURKINA FASO   Overseas Territory) of •UPPER VOL-
                             TA (•HAUTE-VOLTA), one of the ter-
                             ritorial divisions of the federation of
                             •FRENCH WEST AFRICA (Fig. 19).
                             In 1935, however, the colony did not
                             exist. Having been dissolved in Sep-
                             tember 1932, Upper Volta's territory
                             was apportioned among the colonies of
                             IVORY COAST, •FRENCH SUDAN (now
                             MALI), and NIGER (Fig. 4). Upper
                             Volta was reconstituted a separate
                             Overseas Territory of French West
                             Africa in 1947. Became an autonomous

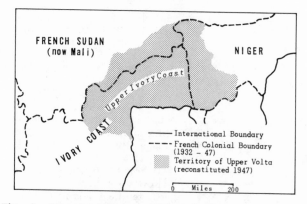

Fig. 4. Boundary Changes Effected by the Dissolution
of the colony of Upper Volta (now Burkina)
in the Period 1932-1947.

member of the French Community in
1958 and called the •VOLTAIC (or
•VOLTA) REPUBLIC (•RÉPUBLIQUE
VOLTAÏQUE) from December 1958 to
March 1959; •REPUBLIC OF [THE]
UPPER VOLTA (•RÉPUBLIQUE DE
HAUTE-VOLTA) was then adopted as
the official name. The republic
achieved full independence on August
5, 1960. In August 1984, the country
was renamed BURKINA (long-form:
BURKINA FASO).

Comment: That part of Upper
Volta's territory attached to the colony
of Ivory Coast (1932 to 1947) was in
1937 constituted an internal district
known as •UPPER IVORY COAST (Fig.
4). In 1947 that district was again
absorbed into the reconstituted territory of Upper Volta.

BURUNDI or REPUBLIC
OF BURUNDI

Formerly the southern division
(•URUNDI) of the Belgian-administered
Trust Territory (originally a mandated
territory under the League of Nations)
of •RUANDA-URUNDI. Became independent as the •KINGDOM OF BURUN-
DI on July 1, 1962 (Fig. 18). Following the deposition of the monarch in

Part Two

1966, the country's official name became REPUBLIC OF BURUNDI. (See
Supp. Note I-D.)

●BURUNDI, KINGDOM OF   See BURUNDI.

Cabinda

Detached province (exclave) of AN-
GOLA located north of the lower Zaire
(Congo) River. (Refer to Fig. 1.)

Comment: In the colonial period,
CABINDA (or KABINDA) was a Portuguese territory administratively
treated as a division of ANGOLA
(●PORTUGUESE WEST AFRICA). Today, Cabinda is an integral administrative division of the independent
PEOPLE'S REPUBLIC OF ANGOLA.

CAMEROON (CAMEROUN)
or REPUBLIC OF
CAMEROON (RÉPUBLIQUE
DU CAMEROUN)

Independent state comprised of the
former mandated (1922-1946) and
Trust Territories (from 1946) of
●FRENCH CAMEROON and the
●SOUTHERN [BRITISH] CAMEROONS
(Fig. 3). French Cameroon also was
an Associated Territory of the French
Union (1946-56).

●FRENCH CAMEROON, the onetime
U.N. trust territory of CAMEROONS
UNDER FRENCH ADMINISTRATION,
was proclaimed the independent state
of CAMEROON (or CAMEROUN) on
January 1, 1960; REPUBLIC OF
CAMEROON became the official name
in March. The Cameroun republic
annexed the former ●SOUTHERN
CAMEROONS in October, 1961, form-
ing the ●FEDERAL REPUBLIC OF
CAMEROON (●RÉPUBLIQUE FÉDÉRALE
DU CAMEROUN). The federation con-
sisted of two states: ●EAST
CAMEROON (the former French
trusteeship) and ●WEST CAMEROON
(the former ●SOUTHERN CAMEROONS)
(Fig. 5).

The country was renamed ●UNITED

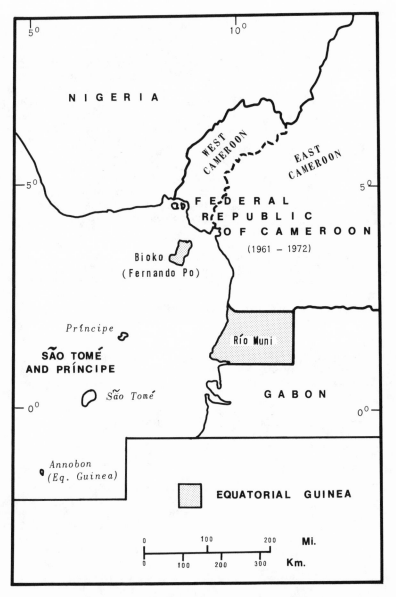

Fig. 5. The Federated Cameroon Republic
(1961-1971), and Equatorial Guinea.

REPUBLIC OF CAMEROON (•RÉPUB-
LIQUE UNIE-DU CAMEROUN) in 1972.
However, in January, 1984, the word
"United" was dropped, and REPUBLIC
OF CAMEROON restored as the official
name. (See Supp. Note I-C.)

Comment: Note that REPUBLIC OF
CAMEROON has been adopted twice as
the official name, first in 1960-61, and
again in 1984. In the earlier period,
however, the name was used briefly,
and then specifically for the republic
which previously had been the •FRENCH
CAMEROON. When the country in 1984
again became the REPUBLIC OF CAME-
ROON, its national territory included
both former (French- and British-
administered) trusteeships which had
been unified since 1961.

•CAMEROON, FEDERAL REPUBLIC OF	See CAMEROON.
•CAMEROON, UNITED REPUBLIC OF	See CAMEROON.
•CAMEROONS UNDER BRITISH ADMINISTRA-TION	See •BRITISH CAMEROONS or Supp. Note I-C.
•CAMEROONS UNDER FRENCH ADMINISTRA-TION	See CAMEROON or Supp. Note I-C.
CAMEROUN	French spelling of CAMEROON (q.v.) sometimes used in English-language publications.
Canary Islands	Spanish archipelago off the north-western coast of Africa (Fig. 16). The Canaries have long been gov-erned as an integral part of the Spanish state. In 1927, the islands were divided into two Spanish provinces, and have been so administered since.

Cape Juby

One of several names used for the former protectorate of •SPANISH SOUTHERN MOROCCO, which was ceded to MOROCCO in 1958 (Fig. 20).

Comment: The name Cape Juby still identifies a headland along the southern coast of Morocco (Fig. 16).

CAPE VERDE or CAPE VERDE ISLANDS; officially REPUBLIC OF CAPE VERDE

Archipelago in the Atlantic Ocean (Fig. 6); formerly a colony (officially designated an "overseas province" in 1951) under Portuguese rule. The CAPE VERDE ISLANDS became an independent republic on July 5, 1975. (See Supp. Note VI-D.)

Comment: Cape Verde (Cap Vert), the westernmost promontory on the African mainland for which the archipelago was named, is in the country of SENEGAL.

CAPE VERDE ISLANDS

See CAPE VERDE.

•CENTRAFRICAINE, EMPIRE

See CENTRAL AFRICAN REPUBLIC.

CENTRAFRICAINE, RÉPUBLIQUE

See CENTRAL AFRICAN REPUBLIC.

CENTRAFRIQUE

See CENTRAL AFRICAN REPUBLIC.

•CENTRAL AFRICAN EMPIRE

See CENTRAL AFRICAN REPUBLIC.

•CENTRAL AFRICAN FEDERATION

See •FEDERATION OF RHODESIA AND NYASALAND.

CENTRAL AFRICAN RE-PUBLIC (CENTRAFRIQUE; RÉPUBLIQUE CENTRAFRI-CAINE)

Formerly known as •UBANGI-SHARI (•OUBANGUI-CHARI) when it was one of the territorial divisions--specifically, an Overseas Territory from 1946--of •FRENCH EQUATORIAL

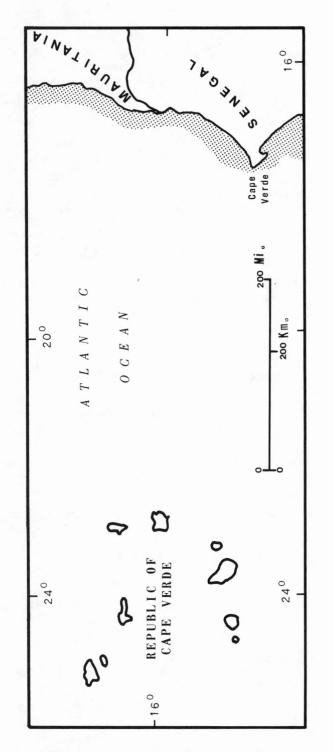

Fig. 6. Cape Verde Islands (Republic of Cape Verde).

AFRICA (Fig. 19). Officially proclaimed the CENTRAL AFRICAN REPUBLIC in December, 1958, when it elected to become an autonomous member state of the French Community (see Supp. Note II-C.) Achieved full independence August 13, 1960.

When a new constitution was adopted in December, 1976, the country was renamed •CENTRAL AFRICAN EMPIRE (•EMPIRE CENTRAFRICAINE). Following the overthrow of Emperor Bokassa's regime in September, 1979, the name CENTRAL AFRICAN REPUBLIC was restored.

Ceuta and Melilla

Diminutive Spanish enclaves along the northern coast of MOROCCO (Fig. 20). Until 1956, the enclaves were surrounded by, but not part of, the protectorate of •SPANISH MOROCCO, having status as plazas de soberanía (places of sovereignty). Thus, when Spanish Morocco was absorbed into the independent KINGDOM OF MOROCCO, Ceuta and Melilla were retained by Spain, and continue to be administered as integral municipalities of the Spanish state.

CHAD or REPUBLIC OF CHAD (RÉPUBLIQUE DU TCHAD)

Formerly one of the territorial divisions (specifically, an Overseas Territory from 1946) of •FRENCH EQUATORIAL AFRICA (Fig. 19). Officially became the REPUBLIC OF CHAD in November 1958 when it elected to become an autonomous member state of the French Community (see Supp. Note II-C). Achieved full independence August 11, 1960.

Comment: In the mid-1970s, a strip of territory along the northern boundary of Chad was annexed by LIBYA. The present government of Chad disputes Libya's claims to the area generally known as the AOZOU (AOUZOU) STRIP (Fig. 13).

Cirenaica

See CYRENAICA, TRIPOLITANIA, and FEZZAN.

CISKEI or
REPUBLIC OF CISKEI

Formerly one of several autonomous "Black (or Tribal) Homelands" established within the REPUBLIC OF SOUTH AFRICA (Fig. 23). Granted full independence by the South African government on December 4, 1981. Ciskei's sovereign status has been formally recognized only by South Africa, but not by other major states of the international community or by the United Nations. (See Supp. Note VIII.)

COMORES

French spelling of COMOROS (COMORO ISLANDS).

COMORO ISLANDS or
COMOROS (COMORES);
officially, FEDERAL
ISLAMIC REPUBLIC OF
THE COMOROS

For more than thirty years, the entire COMORO archipelago (ARCHIPEL DES COMORES), consisting of four principal islands and several islets, was a French colony attached to the colonial administration in MADAGASCAR (Fig. 7). The Comoros were administratively detached from Madagascar in 1946 and made an Overseas Territory (•TERRITOIRE DES COMORES) of the post-war French Union, retaining that status as a member of the French Community after 1958.

On July 6, 1975, three of the islands declared the independence of the •REPUBLIC OF THE COMOROS (•RÉPUBLIQUE DES COMORES); the island of MAYOTTE (MAHORE) did not join the others, preferring to remain under French administration. The French government formally recognized the sovereignty of the (three islands of) Republic of the Comoros in December 1975, but retained control of Mayotte. When a new constitution became effective for the Comoran state in October,

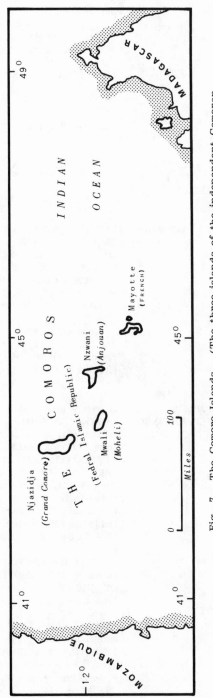

Fig. 7. The Comoro Islands. (The three islands of the independent Comoran state have been renamed: Grande-Comore is now Njazidja; Anjouan is Nzwani; and Moheli is Mwali.)

1978, the country was renamed FED-
ERAL ISLAMIC REPUBLIC OF THE
COMOROS (initially, FEDERAL AND
ISLAMIC ...). (See Supp. Note
VI-C.)

COMOROS   See COMORO ISLANDS.

•COMOROS, REPUBLIC   See COMORO ISLANDS.
OF THE (RÉPUBLIQUE
DES COMORES)

Confederation of Senegambia   Confederal union of the states of
SENEGAL and THE GAMBIA; became
effective February 1, 1982. Intended
to promote cooperation and integration
on certain matters, the confederation
is not a total political union, and each
country retains its sovereign status.

Comment: The term SENEGAMBIA
has long been applied to the general
region consisting of the political territories of SENEGAL and GAMBIA.

CONGO or PEOPLE'S   Formerly known as •MIDDLE CONGO
REPUBLIC OF THE CONGO   (•MOYEN CONGO), a major division
(RÉPUBLIQUE POPULAIRE   (designated an Overseas Territory
DU CONGO)   from 1946) of •FRENCH EQUATORIAL
AFRICA (Fig. 19). Officially renamed
•REPUBLIC OF CONGO (•RÉPUBLIQUE
DU CONGO) in November 1958 when it
opted to become an autonomous mem-
ber within the French Community.
Achieved full independence August 15,
1960. (See Supp. Note II-C.)

Since the adoption of a new constitution in 1970, PEOPLE'S REPUBLIC
OF THE CONGO has been the long-
form name.

Comments: 1. For some years,
especially during the 1960s and early
1970s, the name CONGO-BRAZZAVILLE
served as a convenient short name to
differentiate •REPUBLIC OF CONGO

from the adjacent, then similarly named •[DEMOCRATIC] REPUBLIC OF THE CONGO (also identified as •CONGO-KINSHASA) which became ZAIRE in 1971. Currently, CONGO is understood to be the short-form name for the PEOPLE'S REPUBLIC OF THE CONGO.

2. PEOPLE'S REPUBLIC OF THE CONGO had also been used during 1964-65 as the official name for a short-lived rebel state in the neighboring Democratic Republic of the Congo (now ZAIRE).

•CONGO, DEMOCRATIC REPUBLIC OF THE

See ZAIRE.

•CONGO, REPUBLIC OF THE (RÉPUBLIQUE DU CONGO)

Long-form name adopted by both •MIDDLE CONGO (now PEOPLE'S REPUBLIC OF THE CONGO) and •BELGIAN CONGO (now ZAIRE) upon becoming independent states in 1960. Because of the similarity in the names of the two new independent countries, it was customary to add the name of the capital city to the long- and short-form names: (REPUBLIC OF) •CONGO-BRAZZAVILLE (for Middle Congo), and (REPUBLIC OF THE) •CONGO-LEOPOLDVILLE-- 1960-66, or •CONGO-KINSHASA-- 1966-71 (for Belgian Congo). See "Comment" under entry for ZAIRE.

Congo-Brazzaville

See CONGO.

•CONGO-KINSHASA

See ZAIRE.

•CONGO-LEOPOLDVILLE

See ZAIRE.

Continental Guinea

See EQUATORIAL GUINEA.

•CONTINENTAL (SPAN-   See EQUATORIAL GUINEA.
ISH) GUINEA

CÔTE D'IVOIRE or   See IVORY COAST.
RÉPUBLIQUE DE
CÔTE D'IVOIRE

•CÔTE FRANÇAISE   See DJIBOUTI.
DES SOMALIS

Cyrenaica, Tripolitania,   The present political territory of
and Fezzan   LIBYA was once a North African
                              realm comprising three divisions:
                              Cyrenaica (Cirenaica) in the east,
                              Tripolitania in the northwest, and
                              Fezzan in the south (Fig. 13). The
                              historical divisions were often admin-
                              istered as separate entities, even by
                              the Italians until they created a uni-
                              fied colony of LIBYA (LIBIA) in 1934.

                              Following the withdrawal of the
                              Italians in early 1943, Libia was di-
                              vided; Tripolitania and Cyrenaica
                              were each placed under a British
                              military administration, and most of
                              Fezzan came under French control
                              (Fig. 13). After World War II, con-
                              sideration was given to making each
                              division either a unitary state or a
                              trusteeship. However, the United
                              Nations finally decided the three ter-
                              ritories should be reunited into an
                              independent UNITED KINGDOM OF
                              LIBYA in 1951. (See Supp. Note
                              III-B.)

                              Comment: Even in the modern era,
                              the historical names have often been
                              given to internal political divisions of
                              LIBYA. Today, however, those names
                              are used primarily for identifying gen-
                              eral geographical regions of the coun-
                              try.

•DAHOMEY or REPUBLIC   See BENIN.
OF DAHOMEY (•RÉPUB-
LIQUE DU DAHOMEY)

•DAKAR AND   See SENEGAL.
DEPENDENCIES

DEMOCRATIC AND POPU-   See ALGERIA.
LAR REPUBLIC OF
ALGERIA

•DEMOCRATIC PEOPLE'S   Short-lived coalition government organ-
REPUBLIC OF ANGOLA   ized by two African liberation movements
                           in November 1975 when Portuguese rule
                           ended in ANGOLA. The coalition never
                           received formal recognition as the legal
                           government of the newly independent
                           state of ANGOLA, and ceased to func-
                           tion by early 1976. (See "Comment"
                           under entry for ANGOLA.)

DEMOCRATIC REPUBLIC OF   See SAO TOME AND PRINCIPE.
SAO TOME AND PRINCIPE

•DEMOCRATIC REPUB-   Former long-form name (from 1964 to
LIC OF THE CONGO   1971) of the country now called
                           ZAIRE. The short-form name was
                           •CONGO-LEOPOLDVILLE until 1966,
                           and •CONGO-KINSHASA from 1966 to
                           1971. (See "Comment" under entry
                           for ZAIRE.)

•DEMOCRATIC REPUB-   See SUDAN.
LIC OF THE SUDAN

•DISTRICT OF DAKAR   See SENEGAL.

DJIBOUTI or REPUBLIC   Formerly a French colony (until
OF DJIBOUTI (RÉPUBLIQUE   1946) and Overseas Territory; called
DE DJIBOUTI)   •FRENCH SOMALILAND or •FRENCH
                           SOMALI COAST (•CÔTE FRANÇAISE
                           DES SOMALIS) until 1967, then re-
                           named •FRENCH TERRITORY OF THE
                           AFARS AND THE ISSAS, abbreviated
                           F.T.A.I. (•TERRITOIRE FRANÇAISE
                           DES AFARS ET DES ISSAS, or
                           T.F.A.I.).

                           Achieved independence as a republic

on June 27, 1977; the familiar name
of the port city of DJIBOUTI was
adopted for the national territory
(Fig. 9).

Comment: Prior to World War II,
an alternate spelling, JIBUTI, was
often used for the city, and the
colony at times casually referred to
as the "Jibuti territory."

●EAST CAMEROON   See CAMEROON.

EGYPT or ARAB REPUBLIC   EGYPT, once a British protectorate,
OF EGYPT   was granted independence in 1922; a
                          1936 treaty with Britain resulted in
                          fuller sovereign rights for the Egyp-
                          tian state.

In July, 1952, the monarchy was
overthrown; the new ●REPUBLIC OF
EGYPT was formally proclaimed in
June, 1953. Egypt and Syria were
politically unified in 1958 and adopted
●UNITED ARAB REPUBLIC (U.A.R.)
as the official name of the federated
state. Although the union was dissolved in October 1961, the Egyptians
retained ●UNITED ARAB REPUBLIC
as the conventional name of their national state.

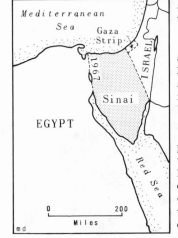

The U.A.R., joining with Libya
and Syria in a ●FEDERATION OF ARAB
REPUBLICS (1971), was renamed the
ARAB REPUBLIC OF EGYPT. (The
federation never developed into a viable political organization, however.)

Comments: 1. During the brief
period when Egypt and Syria were
unified, the Egyptian division was
known as the ●"EGYPTIAN REGION"
or ●"SOUTHERN REGION" of the
●UNITED ARAB REPUBLIC. During
the period 1958-1971, when the state
officially was known as the ●UNITED
ARAB REPUBLIC, Egypt remained a
conventional name in general usage.

Fig. 8.   Sinai Peninsula.

2. The Sinai peninsula of north-eastern EGYPT has generally been recognized an integral part of the modern Egyptian state (Fig. 8). However, from 1967 to 1982, all or part of the Sinai was under Israeli administration, and the Egyptian-Israeli boundary was in a state of flux. Following agreements between the two governments, Israeli forces began their withdrawal from the Sinai; the territory was again fully incorporated into Egypt by 1982. (The status of the diminutive Gaza Strip, originally under Egyptian administration, remains undetermined.)

•EGYPT, REPUBLIC OF   See EGYPT.

•EGYPTIAN REGION   See EGYPT.

•EMPIRE   See CENTRAL AFRICAN REPUBLIC.
CENTRAFRICAINE

•EMPIRE OF ETHIOPIA   Long-form name for ETHIOPIA until
                         the monarchy was overthrown in 1974.

EQUATORIAL GUINEA or   Formerly the colony of •SPANISH
REPUBLIC OF EQUATORIAL   GUINEA (known formally from the
GUINEA   late 1930s as the •SPANISH TERRI-
                          TORIES OF THE GULF OF GUINEA).
                          The overseas entity comprised two
                          principal districts: (1) the mainland
                          territory of RÍO MUNI (also called
                          •CONTINENTAL [SPANISH] GUINEA)
                          and (2) the island of FERNANDO PO
                          (Fig. 5). During 1959-60, the colony
                          was constituted the •SPANISH EQUA-
                          TORIAL REGION with Río Muni and
                          Fernando Po being made Spanish
                          provinces. With increasing autonomy
                          granted the two provinces in 1963,
                          the political entity was renamed
                          EQUATORIAL GUINEA. Complete
                          independence was granted to the
                          REPUBLIC OF EQUATORIAL GUINEA
                          on October 12, 1968.

Following the adoption of a new
constitution in 1973, the island of
Fernando Po was renamed •MACIAS
NGUEMA BIYOGO (also called MACIAS
NGUEMA ISLAND), and then •MASIE
NGUEMA BIYOGO. ANNOBÓN, a
smaller island of Equatorial Guinea,
was renamed •PAGALU. (See Supp.
Note VI-B.)

After the government was overthrown in 1979, Masie Nguema Biyogo
was renamed BIOKO and Pagalu again
became ANNOBÓN.

Comments: 1. For some years,
•SPANISH GUINEA was a term used
primarily for the mainland colony.
However, by the post-World War II
period, SPANISH GUINEA applied to
the collectivity comprising both the
mainland and insular colonies.

2. Several sources suggest the
old name FERNANDO PO (PÓO) is
still a conventional alternate name
for BIOKO.

Eritrea

Territory along the Red Sea coast
which became an Italian colony in the
late nineteenth century (Fig. 9). In
1936, ERITREA was amalgamated with
ETHIOPIA and •ITALIAN SOMALILAND
into an enlarged colony called •ITALIAN
EAST AFRICA (Fig. 11). Following
Italian withdrawal in 1941 and the
dissolution of •ITALIAN EAST AFRICA,
the former colony of ERITREA came
under British military administration.
In 1952, ERITREA became an autonomous territory federated with the
•EMPIRE OF ETHIOPIA; the union was
popularly known as the •FEDERATION
OF ETHIOPIA AND ERITREA. In 1962,
ERITREA lost its autonomous status;
the federation arrangement was terminated, and Eritrea fully absorbed into
the Ethiopian state. (See Supp. Note
III-D.)

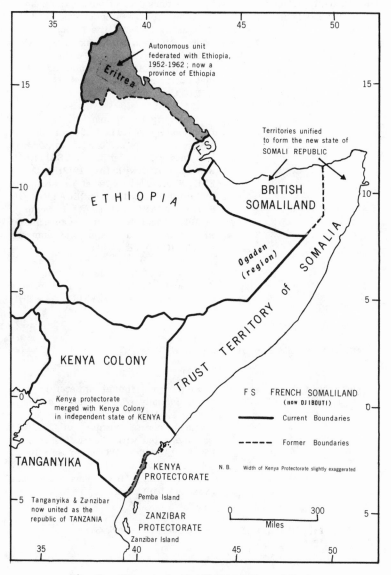

Fig. 9.   Changes in the Political Map of East
Africa and the Horn.

ETHIOPIA,
now officially PEOPLE's
DEMOCRATIC REPUBLIC
OF ETHIOPIA (long-form
name adopted February
1987)

Country also popularly known as
•ABYSSINIA until the 1940s.
ETHIOPIA remained independent during the period of colonial expansion
in Africa, but was conquered by the
Italians in 1935-36; the Ethiopian territory was then amalgamated with the
colonies of •ITALIAN SOMALILAND
and •ERITREA into an enlarged colonial entity called •ITALIAN EAST
AFRICA (see Supp. Note III-C).

Following the Italian withdrawal
from eastern Africa in 1941, Ethiopian
sovereignty was restored. In 1952,
the former Italian colony of ERITREA
was federated with the •EMPIRE OF
ETHIOPIA, creating what was referred
to informally as the •FEDERATION OF
ETHIOPIA AND ERITREA. However,
in 1962, the federation was terminated
when the Eritrean region was annexed
by ETHIOPIA (Fig. 9).

Comment: Until the monarchy was
deposed in 1974, the long-form name
of the country was •EMPIRE OF ETHI-
OPIA.

•ETHIOPIA, EMPIRE OF   See ETHIOPIA.

•ETHIOPIA AND
ERITREA,
FEDERATION OF

Popular name (though apparently
never formally adopted) used in the
period 1952-1962 when the then autonomous coastal territory of ERITREA
was federated with the •EMPIRE OF
ETHIOPIA. The federation was dissolved in 1962 with Eritrea being fully
absorbed into ETHIOPIA as a province.
(See ETHIOPIA and Supp. Note III-D.)

FEDERAL ISLAMIC REPUB-   See COMORO ISLANDS.
LIC OF THE COMOROS

•FEDERAL REPUBLIC   See CAMEROON.
OF CAMEROON

FEDERAL REPUBLIC OF   See NIGERIA.
NIGERIA

•FEDERATION OF   A proposed federation of EGYPT,
ARAB REPUBLICS   LIBYA, and Syria. A constitution
was approved by the three countries
in 1971, and a federal body organized
in 1972. Nevertheless, member states
did not relinquish their sovereignty.
The federation never became a viable
political union, and was eventually
dissolved.

Comment: A union of EGYPT and
LIBYA planned for 1973 was not pur-
sued because of the deteriorating relationship between the two governments.

•FEDERATION OF   See •ETHIOPIA AND ERITREA,
ETHIOPIA AND   FEDERATION OF.
ERITREA

•FEDERATION OF   See •FRENCH WEST AFRICA.
FRENCH WEST AFRICA

•FEDERATION OF MALI   Short-lived federation of the •SU-
DANESE REPUBLIC (SOUDAN) and
SENEGAL, established in April 1959
when both were autonomous member
states within the French Community
(Fig. 19). The federation became
fully independent on June 20, 1960.
However, the federation was dissolved
in August, each division subsequently
being recognized as a unitary republic. The Sudanese Republic was renamed REPUBLIC OF MALI in September. (See Supp. Note II-B.)

•FEDERATION OF   See NIGERIA.
NIGERIA

•FEDERATION OF   Onetime federation of three British
RHODESIA AND   dependencies in Central Africa: the
NYASALAND   British colony of •SOUTHERN

RHODESIA (now ZIMBABWE), and the
protectorates of •NORTHERN RHO-
DESIA (now ZAMBIA) and •NYASA-
LAND (now MALAWI) (Fig. 21). The
Federation, often referred to as the
•CENTRAL AFRICAN FEDERATION,
was constituted in 1953 and dissolved
in 1963. The territories are now in-
dependent countries. (See Supp.
Note V-A.)

Fernando Po (F. Póo)   See EQUATORIAL GUINEA and Supp.
                             Note VI-B.

Fezzan   See CYRENAICA, TRIPOLITANIA,
                             AND FEZZAN; also see Supp. Note
                             III-B.

•FORT OF ST. JOHN   See •SÃO JOÃO BAPTISTA DE AJUDÁ.
THE BAPTIST

•FRENCH CAMEROON(S)   See CAMEROON.
or FRENCH CAMEROUN

•FRENCH CONGO   Name used informally for the terri-
                             tory of •MIDDLE CONGO (now PEO-
                             PLE'S REPUBLIC OF THE CONGO) in
                             •FRENCH EQUATORIAL AFRICA (Fig.
                             19). The name supposedly helped in
                             differentiating the French territory
                             from the neighboring colony of •BEL-
                             GIAN CONGO (now ZAIRE).

                                 Comment: •FRENCH CONGO was
                             also a term used in the early part of
                             this century. At that time, French
                             Congo referred to the group of colo-
                             nies later consolidated as •FRENCH
                             EQUATORIAL AFRICA (q.v.).

•FRENCH EQUATORIAL   Onetime federation comprising the
AFRICA (•AFRIQUE   four French colonies of CHAD, GABON,
ÉQUATORIALE   •MIDDLE CONGO (•MOYEN CONGO),
FRANÇAISE or   and •UBANGI-SHARI (•OUBANGUI-
•A.E.F.)   CHARI) (Fig. 19). •FRENCH
                             CAMEROONS, though having legal

status as a French-administered mandate (see Supp. Note I-C), was often regarded an affiliated unit. By the mid-1930s, the federation had been reorganized into a single colony, the four divisions then designated "regions." Because the new system proved ineffectual, a federal system had been reinstituted by the late 1930s. Under the newly organized French Union of 1946, the four divisions officially were designated "Overseas Territories" within the federation. In 1958, the individual territories opted to become autonomous (though not sovereign) member republics within the new French Community; at that time, Ubangi-Shari and Middle Congo were renamed CENTRAL AFRICAN REPUBLIC and •REPUBLIC OF CONGO (now PEOPLE'S REPUBLIC OF THE CONGO), respectively. The four republics attained full independence in 1960. (See Supp. Notes II-A and II-C.)

•FRENCH GUINEA	See GUINEA.

•FRENCH MOROCCO	Former French protectorate in northwestern Africa. With the protectorate terminated in March, 1956, French Morocco became the independent KINGDOM OF MOROCCO (Fig. 20). The former •NORTHERN ZONE OF THE SPANISH PROTECTORATE IN MOROCCO and the international zone of TANGIER also were incorporated into the new kingdom during 1956. (See Supp. Note IV-A.)

•FRENCH SAHARA	See ALGERIA or •SAHARAN DEPARTMENTS.

•FRENCH SOMALI COAST	See DJIBOUTI.

•FRENCH SOMALILAND	See DJIBOUTI.

•FRENCH SUDAN or   See MALI.
SOUDAN FRANÇAIS

•FRENCH TERRITORY   Former French colony and overseas
OF THE AFARS AND   territory known as •FRENCH SOMALI-
THE ISSAS or F.T.A.I.   LAND until 1967, and from 1967 to
                         1977 as the •FRENCH TERRITORY OF
                         THE AFARS AND THE ISSAS (•TER-
                         RITOIRE FRANÇAISE DES AFARS ET
                         DES ISSAS). The territory became
                         the independent REPUBLIC OF
                         DJIBOUTI in June, 1977 (Fig. 9).

                         Comment: Because of the lengthy
                         name for the small French possession
                         from 1967 to 1977, the abbreviations
                         •F.T.A.I. [English form] and •T.F.A.I.
                         [French form] were sometimes used in
                         articles and maps.

•FRENCH TOGO[LAND]   See TOGO.

•FRENCH WEST AFRICA   Former federation of French territor-
(•AFRIQUE OCCIDEN-   ies (Fig. 19). From 1932 to 1947,
TALE FRANÇAISE or   •FRENCH WEST AFRICA comprised
•AOF); also •FEDERA-   the seven colonies of •DAHOMEY
TION OF FRENCH   (now BENIN), •FRENCH GUINEA
WEST AFRICA   (now GUINEA), •FRENCH SUDAN
                         (now MALI), IVORY COAST, MAURI-
                         TANIA, NIGER, and SENEGAL. In
                         1946, the colonies became "Overseas
                         Territories" of the federation. •UP-
                         PER VOLTA (now BURKINA)--dismem-
                         bered in 1932--was reconstituted as
                         a separate territory in 1947, becoming
                         the eighth Overseas Territory (Fig.
                         4). Though •FRENCH TOGO was a
                         mandated area (trust territory after
                         1946), it was often considered an
                         affiliated unit of French West Africa.

                         Seven of the territories elected to
                         become member states in the newly
                         organized French Community in 1958
                         (French Guinea accepted complete
                         independence), and the weakened
                         federation body was finally dissolved
                         in 1959. In 1960, the separate

territories became independent republics. (See Supp. Notes II-A and
II-B.)

•F.T.A.I.

See •FRENCH TERRITORY OF THE
AFARS AND THE ISSAS.

GABON or GABONESE
REPUBLIC (RÉPUBLIQUE
GABONAISE)

Formerly one of the territorial
divisions--designated an Overseas
Territory from 1946--of •FRENCH
EQUATORIAL AFRICA (Fig. 19).
Officially renamed the GABONESE
REPUBLIC in November, 1958 as an
autonomous member state of the
French Community (see Supp. Note
II-C); Gabon achieved full independ-
ence August 17, 1960.

Comment: The short name will
also be found spelled GABUN or
GABOON, particularly in published
works of earlier periods.

GABONAISE, RÉPUBLIQUE

See GABON.

GABONESE REPUBLIC

See GABON.

Gaboon

See GABON.

Gabun

See GABON.

GAMBIA, also THE
GAMBIA; officially,
REPUBLIC OF THE
GAMBIA

Formerly the British •COLONY AND
PROTECTORATE OF [THE] GAMBIA.
(The colony proper consisted of a
small area at the mouth of the Gambia
River. However, the colony and protectorate were treated as a single administrative entity.)

THE GAMBIA became an independent state on February 18, 1965. When
a new constitution took effect in April
1970, the country's official name became REPUBLIC OF THE GAMBIA.

In February, 1982, The Gambia
joined SENEGAL to form the CONFED-
ERATION OF SENEGAMBIA, but this
did not alter the country's sovereign
status.

GHANA or REPUBLIC OF
GHANA

Independent nation of GHANA founded
March 6, 1957 through the merger of
the British dependency of •GOLD
COAST and the Trust Territory of
•BRITISH TOGOLAND (Figs. 3 and
10). Since the adoption of a new
constitution in 1960, the long-form
name for the country has been RE-
PUBLIC OF GHANA.

Comment: GHANA, the name of a
former West African empire, was
chosen as the name for the first sub-
Saharan nation to achieve independence
in the period after World War II.

•GOLD COAST

Former British "multiple dependency"
consisting of the Gold Coast Colony,
the Ashanti colony, and the protectorate of the Northern Territories
(Fig. 10); the three areas were administered as an amalgamated unit by
the British colonial government. After World War I, the mandated territory (later Trust Territory) of •BRIT-
ISH TOGOLAND was attached administratively with the •GOLD COAST.
The •GOLD COAST, including the
Trust Territory, became the independent nation of GHANA in 1957. (See
Supp. Note I-B.)

Comment: The name •GOLD COAST
applied both to the larger amalgamated
British dependency and to the •GOLD
COAST COLONY, the Crown Colony
founded in the southern coastal area.
Because maps and writings in the
colonial period may not call attention
to the distinction, at times one cannot
be certain if the name •GOLD COAST
is being used for the larger dependency or only the coastal colony.

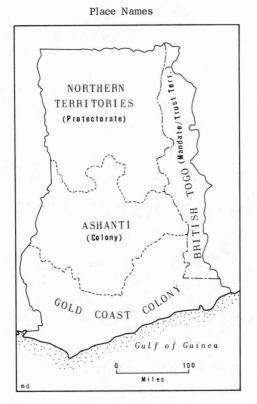

Fig. 10.   The Gold Coast.

•GOLD COAST COLONY   See •GOLD COAST.

Guiné   Portuguese spelling for GUINEA;
                        sometimes given as short-form name
                        in English-language publications for
                        the former •PORTUGUESE GUINEA
                        (now REPUBLIC OF GUINEA-BISSAU).

GUINEA or REPUBLIC OF   Formerly known as •FRENCH GUINEA
GUINEA   (•GUINÉE FRANÇAISE), one of the
                        territorial units of •FRENCH WEST
                        AFRICA (Fig. 19); was a colony un-
                        til 1946, and an Overseas Territory
                        from 1946 to 1958. Attained full in-
                        dependence October 2, 1958 as the
                        REPUBLIC OF GUINEA. In January
                        1979, the country was renamed

•PEOPLE'S REVOLUTIONARY (or
•REVOLUTIONARY PEOPLE'S) REPUB-
LIC OF GUINEA (•RÉPUBLIQUE
POPULAIRE RÉVOLUTIONNAIRE DE
GUINÉE). However, after the mili-
tary coup of April 1984, REPUBLIC
OF GUINEA was restored as the offi-
cial name.

Comment: As the only French
West African territory rejecting membership in the new French Community
in 1958, GUINEA was accorded full
independence immediately. (See Supp.
Notes II-A and II-B.)

Guinea, Continental

Variant name for the mainland province (better known as RÍO MUNI) of
EQUATORIAL GUINEA (q.v.).

•GUINEA, CONTINENTAL
SPANISH

See EQUATORIAL GUINEA.

•GUINEA, PROVINCE OF

See GUINEA-BISSAU.

GUINEA-BISSAU or
REPUBLIC OF GUINEA-
BISSAU

Former Portuguese colony (formally
designated as "overseas province" in
1951) known as •PORTUGUESE
GUINEA or as •PROVINCE OF GUINEA.
Independence was declared unilateral-
ly by leaders of the nationalist movement (the PAIGC) in September, 1973,
with the PAIGC organization accorded
recognition by several countries and
the U.N. The independence of
GUINEA-BISSAU was recognized by
Portugal on September 10, 1974.

Comment: Although GUINEA-
BISSAU was made the official name of
the independent republic, it was used
years before by the PAIGC movement
and its supporters when referring to
the political territory. (See Supp.
Note VI-D and entry for •PORTU-
GUESE AFRICA.)

GUINÉE

French spelling for GUINEA (q.v.), but occasionally used in English language publications for former •FRENCH GUINEA and present REPUBLIC OF GUINEA.

•GUINÉE FRANÇAISE

See GUINEA.

•HAUTE-VOLTA or •RÉPUBLIQUE DE HAUTE-VOLTA

See BURKINA.

•HIGH COMMISSION TERRITORIES

Former term for three British territories in southern Africa: •BASUTO-LAND (now LESOTHO), •BECHUANA-LAND PROTECTORATE (now BOTS-WANA), and SWAZILAND (Fig. 22). Until 1964, the three territories--also referred to as "the Protectorates"--were under the general authority of a British High Commissioner resident in the •UNION (now REPUBLIC) OF SOUTH AFRICA. The office of High Commissioner was dissolved in 1964. Following a transitional period with extended powers of self-government, each territory was granted full independence. (See Supp. Note V-C.)

•IFNI

Former small Spanish colony along the coast of northwestern Africa (Fig. 20). Was one of two major divisions of •SPANISH WEST AFRICA from 1946 to 1958, and then given status as a Spanish Overseas Province. The Spanish relinquished their claim to Ifni in 1969, and the territory was annexed by MOROCCO. (See Supp. Note IV-C.)

•INTERNATIONAL ZONE OF TANGIER

See TANGIER and Supp. Note IV-A.

ISLAMIC REPUBLIC OF MAURITANIA

See MAURITANIA.

Part Two

•ITALIAN EAST AFRICA
or •ITALIAN EMPIRE
OF EAST AFRICA

Following the conquest of ETHIOPIA (•ABYSSINIA) in 1935-36, the Italian government consolidated its possessions in eastern Africa, forming the large overseas dependency called •ITALIAN EAST AFRICA. As the principal colonial territory of Mussolini's Fascist Empire, Italian East Africa welded the newly acquired Ethiopian territory with the colonies of ERITREA and •ITALIAN SOMALILAND (Fig. 11).

Following the withdrawal of Italian forces from the region in 1941, the Italian East African colony was disestablished. The Ethiopian monarchy was restored, while the British took over administration of ERITREA and the former •ITALIAN SOMALILAND until the United Nations agreed upon the disposition of those territories some years later. (See Supp. Notes III-C and III-D.)

•ITALIAN EMPIRE OF
EAST AFRICA

See ITALIAN EAST AFRICA or Supp. Note III-C.

•ITALIAN SOMALILAND

Italian colony established in the Horn of Africa in the late nineteenth century. Governed as a separate dependency until 1936 when it was joined with ETHIOPIA and ERITREA to form •ITALIAN EAST AFRICA (Fig. 11). Following the Italian loss and subsequent dissolution of •ITALIAN EAST AFRICA in 1941, the former •ITALIAN SOMALILAND was placed under British administration. In 1950, the U.N. reconstituted the onetime colony as the •TRUST TERRITORY OF SOMALILAND UNDER ITALIAN ADMINISTRATION. The Trust Territory became independent in July 1960, and united with former •BRITISH SOMALILAND to form the new •SOMALI REPUBLIC (now SOMALI DEMOCRATIC REPUBLIC). (See SOMALIA and Supp. Notes III-A and III-D.)

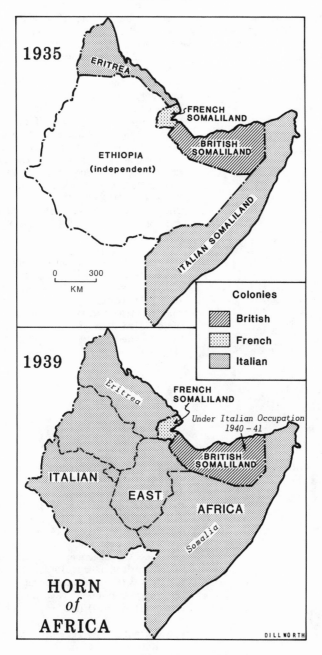

Fig. 11.

IVORY COAST or REPUBLIC OF THE IVORY COAST (RÉPUBLIQUE DE CÔTE D'IVOIRE)

Formerly one of the territorial divisions of the federation of •FRENCH WEST AFRICA, as a colony until 1946, and an Overseas Territory from 1946 to 1958. In 1947, a portion of its territory was detached and incorporated into •UPPER VOLTA (now BURKINA) which was being reconstituted as a major division of the federation (Figs. 19 and 4). In December 1958, IVORY COAST became an autonomous member state of the French Community and adopted REPUBLIC OF THE IVORY COAST (RÉPUBLIQUE DE CÔTE D'IVOIRE) as the official name. The republic achieved full independence on August 7, 1960. (See Supp. Note II-B.)

Comment: A portion of Upper Volta's territory was incorporated with the Ivory Coast from 1932 to 1947. That attached area was set apart in 1937 and made a special administrative district (within Ivory Coast) called •UPPER IVORY COAST (Fig. 4).

Jibuti

See DJIBOUTI.

Kabinda

See CABINDA.

•KATANGA

Province of the former colony of •BELGIAN CONGO (Fig. 12). In July 1960, the province seceded from the newly independent •REPUBLIC OF THE CONGO (now ZAIRE), and the sovereignty of KATANGA was proclaimed by local leaders. The Katangan secessionist government functioned until January, 1963 when the territory was again incorporated into the Congo republic. (See Supp. Notes VII-A and VII-B.)

Comment: The region of the onetime Katanga province has since been renamed Shaba.

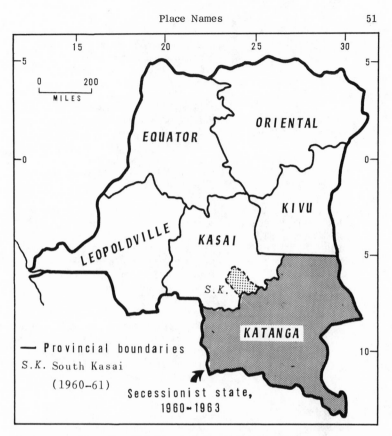

Fig. 12. Provinces of the Republic of the
Congo (now Zaire) in 1960, and
the Secessionist States of
Katanga and South Kasai.

KENYA or REPUBLIC
OF KENYA

After 1920, the British dependency known formally as
•KENYA COLONY AND PROTECTOR-
ATE comprised the British colony of
KENYA and a narrow coastal strip
(•KENYA PROTECTORATE); the protectorate was legally within the Sultan
of Zanzibar's domain, but administratively integrated with Kenya Colony
(Fig. 9). Before KENYA became independent on December 12, 1963, the
Sultan of Zanzibar had agreed to re-
nounce his claim to the coastal strip,
thereby permitting its full absorption

into the Kenyan state. Following
constitutional changes, the country
officially became the REPUBLIC OF
KENYA in December, 1964.

•KENYA COASTAL STRIP	See •KENYA PROTECTORATE.

•KENYA COLONY AND PROTECTORATE	See KENYA.

•KENYA PROTECTORATE or KENYA COASTAL STRIP

Narrow coastal strip in KENYA extending from the KENYA-•TANGANYIKA (now TANZANIA) boundary to the mouth of the Tana River, and including the Lamu archipelago; technically remained part of the ZANZIBAR protectorate until KENYA became independent (Fig. 9). The coastal strip, approximately ten miles wide, had been administered by the British as part of •KENYA COLONY, but was fully incorporated into the new Kenyan state in 1963.

Comment: The boundaries and special status of the coastal strip were infrequently noted on maps in the colonial period.

•KINGDOM OF BURUNDI	See BURUNDI.
KINGDOM OF LESOTHO	See LESOTHO.
KINGDOM OF MOROCCO	See MOROCCO.
KINGDOM OF SWAZILAND	See SWAZILAND.

LESOTHO or KINGDOM OF LESOTHO

Formerly the British •HIGH COMMISSION TERRITORY of •BASUTOLAND until 1964, then becoming a self-governing dependency for a brief period. Granted full independence

as the KINGDOM OF LESOTHO on
October 4, 1966. (See Supp. Note
V-C.)

LIBERIA or REPUBLIC OF   Established as an independent repub-
LIBERIA   lic on July 26, 1847. Despite en-
                                croachments on its territory by Euro-
                                pean powers, Liberia retained its
                                sovereign status during the period
                                of active colonial expansion in Africa
                                in the late 19th century.

Libia   See LIBYA.

LIBYA or LIBYAN ARAB   Former Italian colony (after 1912);
JAMAHIRIYA; officially,   the provinces of CYRENAICA
SOCIALIST PEOPLE'S   (CIRENAICA) and TRIPOLITANIA,
LIBYAN ARAB   originally administered separately,
JAMAHIRIYA   were constituted a single colony
                                (LIBYA or •ITALIAN LIBIA) in 1934.
                                In 1939, the provinces of northern
                                Libya were incorporated into the
                                Italian state (Fig. 13); the southern
                                part remained a military district.
                                Following the Italian withdrawal from
                                Libya in 1943, TRIPOLITANIA and
                                CYRENAICA came under British mili-
                                tary administration, and the southern
                                zone (FEZZAN) under French admin-
                                istration (Fig. 13).

                                The three areas were reunited on
                                December 24, 1951, as the independ-
                                ent •UNITED KINGDOM OF LIBYA,
                                but the name was shortened to •KING-
                                DOM OF LIBYA in 1963 after the fed-
                                eral system had been abolished. When
                                the monarchy was overthrown in 1969,
                                the country became the •LIBYAN ARAB
                                REPUBLIC. In 1977, the denomination
                                was officially changed to SOCIALIST
                                PEOPLE'S LIBYAN ARAB JAMAHIRIYA.
                                (See Supp. Notes III-A and III-B.)

                                Comments: 1. The alternate
                                spelling, LIBIA, was used frequently
                                in English-language maps and publi-
                                cations until the 1940s.

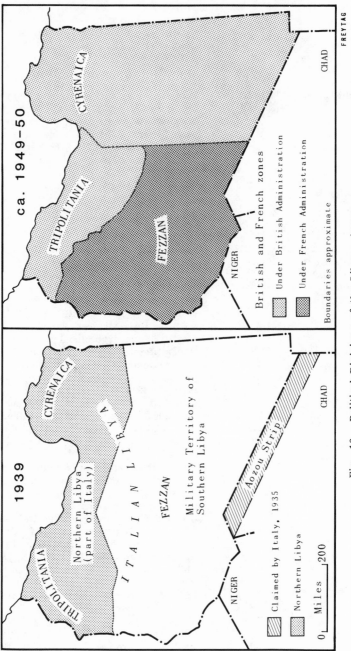

Fig. 13. Political Divisions of the Libyan Area.

2. Since the mid-1970s, Libya has occupied the AOZOU (AOUZOU) STRIP in northern CHAD. The government of Chad does not recognize Libya's claims to that territory (Fig. 13).

•LIBYA, KINGDOM OF

Long-form name of the independent state of LIBYA in the period 1963-1969. See LIBYA.

•LIBYA, UNITED KINGDOM OF

Long-form name for LIBYA from its independence in 1952 until 1963. See LIBYA.

•LIBYAN ARAB REPUBLIC

Long form title adopted for LIBYA after the monarchy was overthrown in 1969; name continued in use until 1977.

•MACIAS NGUEMA BIYOGO or •MACIAS NGUEMA ISLAND

See EQUATORIAL GUINEA or Supp. Note VI-B.

MADAGASCAR or DEMO-CRATIC REPUBLIC OF MADAGASCAR (RÉPUB-LIQUE DÉMOCRATIQUE DE MADAGASCAR)

MADAGASCAR, largest of the islands adjacent to Africa, had been a French colony (Madagascar and Dependencies) from 1896. After the fall of France in 1940, Madagascar was dominated by the Vichy government. However, British forces seized control of the island during 1942, and then transferred it to the Free (Fighting) French authorities. In 1946, Madagascar became an Overseas Territory of the French Union.

Madagascar was among the overseas areas which approved (by referendum) the French Constitution of 1958; the island became a member-state--renamed •MALAGASY REPUBLIC --of the newly structured French Community in October 1958. The republic achieved full independence on June 26, 1960. (See Supp. Note VI-C.)

In December, 1975, DEMOCRATIC
REPUBLIC OF MADAGASCAR was
adopted as the official name for the
island-state.

Comments: 1. While •MALAGASY
REPUBLIC (•RÉPUBLIQUE MALGACHE)
was the official name from 1958 to
1975, MADAGASCAR continued to
serve as a conventional name, both
for the island and (as a variant name)
for the political state.

2. Until 1946, the colony of the
COMORO ISLANDS was attached administratively to Madagascar (Fig. 7).

Mahore   See MAYOTTE.

Mainland Tanzania   See •TANGANYIKA and TANZANIA.

•MALAGASY REPUBLIC   See MADAGASCAR.

MALAWI or REPUBLIC OF   Formerly the British protectorate of
MALAWI   •NYASALAND; from 1953 to 1963, the
                                    protectorate was one of three British
                                    Central Africa areas comprising the
                                    •FEDERATION OF RHODESIA AND
                                    NYASALAND (Fig. 21). On July 6,
                                    1964, the state achieved full inde-
                                    pendence, adopting the name MALAWI;
                                    in July 1966, a new constitution was
                                    adopted and the country proclaimed
                                    the REPUBLIC OF MALAWI. (See
                                    Supp. Note V-A.)

                                    Comment: Most of Lake Nyasa
                                    (now also called Lake Malawi) lies
                                    within the country of MALAWI. How-
                                    ever, an Anglo-Portuguese agreement
                                    signed in 1954 extended the western
                                    boundary of neighboring MOZAMBIQUE
                                    to include a portion of the lake. To-
                                    day, part of the lake is still recog-
                                    nized as falling within Mozambique's
                                    national territory (Fig. 21).

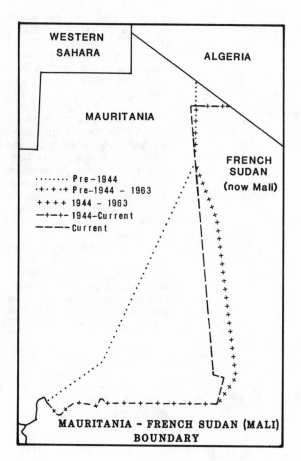

Fig. 14.

•MALGACHE,   See MADAGASCAR.
  RÉPUBLIQUE

MALI or REPUBLIC OF   Formerly known as •FRENCH SUDAN
MALI (RÉPUBLIQUE DU   (•SOUDAN FRANÇAIS), one of the
MALI)   territorial divisions of •FRENCH WEST
                        AFRICA which was a colony until
                        1946 and an Overseas territory from
                        1946 to 1958.

                            In 1944, part of the western

region of French Sudan was transferred to the colony of Mauritania
(Fig. 14). Another portion of French
Sudan was taken in 1947 and incorporated into the reconstituted territory
of •UPPER VOLTA (now BURKINA)
(see Fig. 4).

•FRENCH SUDAN was renamed
•SUDANESE REPUBLIC (•RÉPUBLIQUE
SOUDANAISE) when it became an
autonomous member state of the
French Community in December 1958.
The Sudanese Republic united with
neighboring SENEGAL (also an autonomous republic in the French Community) to form the •FEDERATION OF
MALI; the federation attained full
independence on June 20, 1960.

Following the federation's breakup
in August 1960, the Sudanese government proclaimed its independence on
September 22 as the REPUBLIC OF
MALI. (See Supp. Note II-B.)

Comment: In English language
publications, •SOUDAN (French spelling) also appeared as a short form
variant for •FRENCH SUDAN (•TER-
RITOIRE DU SOUDAN) and the
•SUDANESE REPUBLIC.

•MALI, FEDERATION OF (or •MALI FEDERATION)	See FEDERATION OF MALI.
MAROC	French name for MOROCCO (q.v.).
•MASIE NGUEMA BIYOGO or •MASIE NGUEMA ISLAND	See EQUATORIAL GUINEA.
MAURITANIA or ISLAMIC REPUBLIC OF MAURITANIA (RÉPUBLIQUE ISLAMIQUE DE MAURITANIE)	Independent republic which had been a colony (until 1946) and Overseas Territory of •FRENCH WEST AFRICA. Mauritania was enlarged in 1944 when part of the •FRENCH SUDAN colony

(now MALI) was transferred to it
(Fig. 14). Present long-form name
adopted in 1958 when Mauritania became a self-governing member-state
of the French Community; granted
full independence November 28, 1960.
(See Supp. Note II-B.)

From 1976 to 1979, Mauritania controlled the southern portion of WEST-
ERN SAHARA (the former •SPANISH
SAHARA) (Fig. 16). After the 1978
military coup in Mauritania, the new
government renounced its claims to
the Western Saharan territory, and
withdrew its forces in 1979. (See
WESTERN SAHARA for a review on
subsequent developments of that
region.)

Comment: Although Mauritania was
one of the principal divisions of French
West Africa, it was nonetheless regarded as an appendage of the neighboring colony of SENEGAL. Mauritania did not have an internal administrative capital until 1957.

MAURITANIE   French spelling of MAURITANIA (q.v.).

MAYOTTE   One of the four principal islands of
                            the Comoro archipelago (Fig. 7).
                            The COMORO ISLANDS were under
                            French administration until July, 1975
                            when three of the islands unilaterally
                            declared their independence as the
                            •REPUBLIC OF THE COMOROS (now
                            FEDERAL ISLAMIC REPUBLIC OF THE
                            COMOROS). MAYOTTE, the fourth
                            island, remains under French admin-
                            istration with the special status of a
                            "territorial collectivity." (See Supp.
                            Note VI-C.)

                            Comment: Each of the Comoro
                            Islands, including Mayotte, was re-
                            named by the Comoran Republic.
                            The name MAHORE was adopted for
                            Mayotte, although it is not part of

the Comoran state. The French government continues to use MAYOTTE
as the official name.

"Mbini"   Name given in some sources for the
                                 mainland component (RÍO MUNI) of
                                 EQUATORIAL GUINEA. However,
                                 adoption of MBINI as either an offi-
                                 cial or an alternate mainland desig-
                                 nation could not be documented.

Melilla   See CEUTA AND MELILLA.

•MIDDLE CONGO   See CONGO.

•MINING STATE (OF   See •SOUTH KASAI and Supp. Note
SOUTH KASAI)   VII-A.

MOÇAMBIQUE   See MOZAMBIQUE.

MOROCCO or KINGDOM   Independent kingdom established in
OF MOROCCO (MAROC)   1956, beginning with the termination
                                 of the protectorate of •FRENCH
                                 MOROCCO in March, then followed
                                 by annexations of the northern zone
                                 of the •SPANISH PROTECTORATE IN
                                 MOROCCO (•SPANISH MOROCCO) in
                                 April, and the •TANGIER ZONE in
                                 October (Fig. 20). Morocco's national
                                 territory was enlarged in 1958 by ab-
                                 sorbing the •SOUTHERN ZONE OF THE
                                 SPANISH PROTECTORATE (•SPANISH
                                 SOUTHERN MOROCCO) and again in
                                 1969 with the addition of Spain's small
                                 coastal province of •IFNI. Moroccan
                                 political territory was extended further
                                 in 1976 when the northern and central
                                 regions of former •SPANISH SAHARA
                                 were annexed. When MAURITANIA
                                 relinquished the southern portion of
                                 the former Spanish Sahara in 1979,
                                 Moroccan forces promptly occupied
                                 that region. (See Supp. Notes IV-A
                                 and IV-C, and Fig. 16.)

Comment: The legality of MOROC-
CO's annexation and occupation of the
former Spanish Sahara (now referred
to as WESTERN SAHARA) has been
challenged. (See WESTERN SAHARA.)

•MOYEN CONGO   See CONGO.

MOZAMBIQUE (also   Former Portuguese territory also
MOÇAMBIQUE) or   known as •PORTUGUESE EAST AF-
PEOPLE'S REPUBLIC   RICA. Was administered as an over-
OF MOZAMBIQUE   seas possession or colony, then given
                       official status as a Portuguese Over-
                       seas Territory in 1951; became an
                       autonomous Portuguese state in 1972.
                       Achieved full independence on June 25,
                       1975, adopting PEOPLE'S REPUBLIC
                       OF MOZAMBIQUE as the official name.

NAMIBIA or SOUTH WEST   Former German protectorate which be-
AFRICA (SWA)   came a mandated area under the
                       League of Nations after World War I
                       (Fig. 17). The •UNION (REPUBLIC
                       since 1961) OF SOUTH AFRICA ad-
                       ministered the mandate. After World
                       War II, the government of SOUTH
                       AFRICA refused to place SOUTH WEST
                       AFRICA under the new trusteeship
                       system of the United Nations. The
                       U.N. in 1966 ostensibly terminated
                       the mandate, intending to take over
                       administration of the territory. The
                       South African government argued the
                       U.N. resolution was not binding, and
                       retained administrative authority in
                       Namibia. In June 1968, the U.N.
                       adopted NAMIBIA as the official name
                       for the territory. Since that time,
                       NAMIBIA and SOUTH WEST AFRICA
                       have been used interchangeably, some-
                       times even together (e.g., SOUTH
                       WEST AFRICA [SWA] /NAMIBIA).
                       Nevertheless, NAMIBIA has been in-
                       creasingly accepted as the convention-
                       al name. (See Supp. Note I-E and
                       WALVIS BAY.)

NIGER or REPUBLIC OF [THE] NIGER (RÉPUBLIQUE DU NIGER)

Formerly one of the territorial divisions of the federation of •FRENCH WEST AFRICA, as a colony until 1946, and an Overseas Territory from 1946 to 1958 (Fig. 19). In 1947, a portion of NIGER's territory was transferred to •UPPER VOLTA (now BURKINA FASO), a previously dismembered colony then being reconstituted (Fig. 4). Niger officially became the RE-PUBLIC OF [THE] NIGER in December 1958, when it joined the French Community as an autonomous member state; full independence was attained August 3, 1960. (See Supp. Note II-B.)

NIGERIA or FEDERAL REPUBLIC OF NIGERIA

Formerly the British •COLONY AND PROTECTORATE OF NIGERIA. The Colony consisted of a small area along the coast of southwestern Nigeria; the Protectorate was comprised of two (three after 1939) Provinces. Nevertheless, all of Nigeria was under a centralized administration. In the 1920s, the mandated area of •BRITISH (NORTHERN and SOUTHERN) CAME-ROONS was also integrated into Nigeria's colonial administration (Fig. 3).

With the enactment of the 1954 constitution, the British dependency officially became the •FEDERATION OF NIGERIA, and the internal divisions were designated "Regions" (Fig. 2). In addition, •SOUTHERN CAMER-OONS was assigned special status as a "quasi-province" within the federation. The Federation of Nigeria achieved full independence on October 1, 1960. (However, the British Cameroons, still technically a Trusteeship, had been detached and was no longer affiliated with the Nigerian state.)

Territory was added to Nigeria in October 1961 with the annexation of the former NORTHERN CAMEROONS (see Supp. Note I-C). A new constitution in 1964 resulted in the country being renamed FEDERAL REPUBLIC OF NIGERIA.

In May 1967, the Eastern Region (as then constituted) seceded from the federal state, proclaiming its independence as the •REPUBLIC OF BIAFRA. That action precipitated a civil war that continued until January 1970. The secessionist territory was again incorporated into the federal state, thereby restoring Nigeria's territorial integrity. (See Supp. Notes VII-A and VII-C.)

Comment: FEDERAL REPUBLIC OF NIGERIA has been the official name since 1964 except for a few months during 1966 when the state was called the •REPUBLIC OF NIGERIA. At the time some leaders sought (not successfully) to reduce regional authority by instituting a strong centralized government.

•NIGERIA, FEDERATION OF	See NIGERIA.
•NIGERIA, REPUBLIC OF	See NIGERIA.
•NORTHERN [BRITISH] CAMEROONS	See •BRITISH CAMEROONS or Supp. Note I-C.
•NORTHERN RHODESIA	See ZAMBIA.
•NORTHERN ZONE OF THE SPANISH PROTEC-TORATE IN MOROCCO	See SPANISH MOROCCO and Supp. Note IV-C.
•NYASALAND	See MALAWI.
•OUBANGUI-CHARI	See CENTRAL AFRICAN REPUBLIC.

PAIGC   Abbreviation for PARTIDO AFRICANO
                                      DA INDEPENDÊNCIA DA GUINÉ E
                                      CABO VERDE (AFRICAN PARTY FOR
                                      THE INDEPENDENCE OF GUINEA-
                                      BISSAU AND CAPE VERDE). (See
                                      Supp. Note VI-D.)

•PAGALU   See ANNOBON.

Partido Africano da   See Supp. Note VI-D.
Independência da Guiné
e Cabo Verde or PAIGC

PEOPLE'S DEMOCRATIC   See ALGERIA.
REPUBLIC OF ALGERIA

PEOPLE'S REPUBLIC   See ANGOLA.
OF ANGOLA

PEOPLE'S REPUBLIC   See BENIN.
OF BENIN

•PEOPLE'S REPUBLIC   See ZANZIBAR and TANZANIA.
OF ZANZIBAR

•PEOPLE'S REVOLU-   See GUINEA.
TIONARY REPUBLIC
OF GUINEA

•PORTUGUESE AFRICA   Collective term for the former Portu-
                                      guese possessions in the African
                                      realm, viz., the mainland territories
                                      of MOZAMBIQUE, ANGOLA, and
                                      •PORTUGUESE GUINEA (now GUINEA-
                                      BISSAU), and the offshore dependen-
                                      cies of CAPE VERDE ISLANDS (now
                                      REPUBLIC OF CAPE VERDE) and SAO
                                      TOME AND PRINCIPE. Never having
                                      had a consistent designation of status
                                      through the years, each territory was
                                      formally made an Overseas Province
                                      in 1951. Each province was treated
                                      as an integral division of the Portuguese

state and administered by a Governor
or Governor-General. In 1972 ANGOLA
and MOZAMBIQUE became autonomous
Portuguese "states." All the Portuguese possessions achieved full independence during 1974-75.

•PORTUGUESE EAST   See MOZAMBIQUE.
  AFRICA

•PORTUGUESE GUINEA   See GUINEA-BISSAU.

•PORTUGUESE WEST   Alternate name used for ANGOLA
  AFRICA   (q.v.) in the colonial period.

Príncipe   See SAO TOME AND PRINCIPE.

•PROVINCE OF GUINEA   See GUINEA-BISSAU.

•PROVINCE OF SAHARA   See WESTERN SAHARA and •SAHARA,
                          PROVINCE OF.

•REPUBLIC OF EGYPT   See EGYPT.

REPUBLIC OF THE SUDAN   See SUDAN.

RÉPUBLIQUE CENTRAFRI-   See CENTRAL AFRICAN REPUBLIC.
CAINE

RÉPUBLIQUE DE GUINÉE   See GUINEA.

•RÉPUBLIQUE DE   See BURKINA.
  HAUTE-VOLTA

RÉPUBLIQUE DÉMO-   See MADAGASCAR.
CRATIQUE DE
MADAGASCAR

•RÉPUBLIQUE DES   See COMORO ISLANDS.
  COMORES

•RÉPUBLIQUE FÉDÉRALE   See CAMEROON.
  DU CAMEROUN

RÉPUBLIQUE ISLAMIQUE   See MAURITANIA.
DE MAURITANIE

•RÉPUBLIQUE   See MADAGASCAR.
  MALGACHE

RÉPUBLIQUE POPULAIRE   See BENIN.
DU BENIN

RÉPUBLIQUE POPULAIRE   See CONGO.
DU CONGO

•RÉPUBLIQUE   See GUINEA.
  POPULAIRE ET
  RÉVOLUTIONNAIRE
  DE GUINÉE

•RÉPUBLIQUE-UNIE   See CAMEROON.
  DU CAMEROUN

•REVOLUTIONARY   Long-form name (English translation)
  PEOPLE'S REPUBLIC   used by the U.N. and some other in-
  OF GUINEA   ternational organizations for GUINEA
                           (now officially REPUBLIC OF GUINEA)
                           in the period 1979-1984.

•RHODESIA   See ZIMBABWE or Supp. Note V-B.

•RHODESIA AND   See •FEDERATION OF RHODESIA AND
  NYASALAND, FED-   NYASALAND and Supp. Note V-A.
  ERATION OF

Río de Oro   Term once generally applied to all
                           Spanish overseas territories in

northwestern Africa including the colony of Río de Oro and the "occupied zone" of Saguia el Hamra (Fig. 20); the region was also referred to as "Spanish (Western) Sahara."

Comment: Although •SPANISH SAHARA (i.e., RÍO DE ORO and SAGUIA EL HAMRA) was decreed (1946) a constituent part of the new overseas entity of •SPANISH WEST AFRICA, many maps would continue to simply label the entire region "Río de Oro." (See WESTERN SAHARA and Supp. Note IV-C.)

Río Muni

Mainland division of EQUATORIAL GUINEA (q.v.).

RPA

Commonly used abbreviation for Republica Popular de Angola, the Portuguese long-form name for the PEOPLE'S REPUBLIC OF ANGOLA.

•RUANDA

See RWANDA.

•RUANDA-URUNDI or •TERRITORY OF RUANDA-URUNDI

Territory formerly under Belgian administration, first as a mandate under the League of Nations (mandate awarded to Belgium after World War I), and from 1946 as a Trust Territory under the United Nations (Fig. 17). In July 1962, the Trusteeship status was terminated by the U.N. and the territory was partitioned; the northern (•RUANDA) and southern (•URUNDI) divisions thereupon became the independent states of RWANDA and BURUNDI, respectively. (See Supp. Notes I-A and I-D, and Fig. 18.)

Comment: Despite the special status of Ruanda-Urundi, the Belgian government in 1925 tied it administratively with the colony of •BELGIAN CONGO. The territory was so administered until 1960 when the Belgian Congo became independent.

RWANDA; officially
REPUBLIC OF RWANDA or
RWANDESE REPUBLIC

Formerly the northern division
(•RUANDA) of the Belgian-
administered Trust Territory (a man-
dated territory under the League of
Nations until 1946) of •RUANDA-
URUNDI. Achieved independence on
July 1, 1962, becoming the REPUBLIC
OF RWANDA. (See Supp. Note I-D
and Fig. 18.)

RWANDESE REPUBLIC

See RWANDA.

SADR

See SAHARAN ARAB DEMOCRATIC
REPUBLIC or WESTERN SAHARA.

Saguia el Hamra

See •SPANISH WEST AFRICA.

•SAHARA, PROVINCE
OF

Official name for •SPANISH SAHARA
from 1958 to 1975 when it held status
as a province of Spain. See WESTERN
SAHARA.

Saharan [Saharawi] Arab
Democratic Republic
(SADR)

Name adopted (1976) for the disputed
territory of WESTERN SAHARA (formerly •SPANISH SAHARA) by the
Polisario Front (Popular Front for the
Liberation of Saguia el Hamra and Río
de Oro). The Polisario movement
seeks full sovereignty for the territory which is currently occupied by
Moroccan forces (Fig. 16). (See
WESTERN SAHARA or Supp. Note
IV-C.)

•SAHARAN DEPART-
MENTS or •FRENCH
SAHARA

Term referring to the southern region
of ALGERIA during the period 1957-
1962 (Fig. 20). The newly constituted Saharan Departments of Oases
and Saoura were intended to function
as a separate political entity within
the French Community. The Saharan
area was incorporated into the Algerian
state when it achieved independence in
1962. (See Supp. Note IV-B.)

Saharawi Arab Democratic Republic	See SAHARAN ARAB DEMOCRATIC REPUBLIC or WESTERN SAHARA.
•SÃO JOÃO BAPTISTA DE AJUDÁ	A former Portuguese enclave (including the •FORT OF ST. JOHN THE BAPTIST) situated in the coastal town of Ouidah (AJUDÁ in Portuguese) in the French colony of •DAHOMEY. The 11-acre parcel was administered with the Portuguese dependency of SAO TOME AND PRINCIPE. Dahomey (now BENIN) became independent in 1960, and Dahomean forces seized and annexed the enclave the next year.
São Tomé	See SAO TOME AND PRINCIPE.
SAO TOME AND PRINCIPE or DEMOCRATIC REPUBLIC OF SAO TOME AND PRINCIPE	Formerly a Portuguese colony and overseas province comprising the islands of SÃO TOMÉ and PRÍNCIPE (Fig. 5). The insular entity was granted local autonomy in 1973, and became an independent republic on July 12, 1975. (See Supp. Note VI-A.) Comment: SÃO JOÃO BAPTISTA DE AJUDÁ, a small Portuguese enclave in the French mainland colony of •DAHOMEY, was also administered with SAO TOME AND PRINCIPE. The enclave was incorporated into •DAHOMEY (later renamed BENIN) in 1961.
SENEGAL or REPUBLIC OF SENEGAL (RÉPUBLIQUE DU SÉNÉGAL)	Formerly one of the territorial divisions of the federation of •FRENCH WEST AFRICA, as a colony until 1946, and as an Overseas Territory from 1946 to 1958. Officially became the REPUBLIC OF SENEGAL, an autonomous member state of the French Community, in November 1958. In April 1959, Senegal joined with

the •SUDANESE REPUBLIC (now
MALI), another member of the French
Community, to form the •MALI FEDER-
ATION (Fig. 19); the Federation attained full independence on June 20,
1960. On August 20, Senegal withdrew from the Federation, and thereupon declared sovereign status. (See
Supp. Note II-B.)

In 1982, SENEGAL joined THE
GAMBIA to form the CONFEDERATION
OF SENEGAMBIA, though under this
arrangement, each country retains its
sovereignty.

Comment: From the mid-1920s, the
city of Dakar (the federation capital)
and nearby areas formed the special
•DISTRICT OF DAKAR or •DAKAR
AND DEPENDENCIES (Circonscription
de Dakar et Dépendances). Though
located within Senegalese territory,
the District was not administered as
part of the colony.

Senegambia

See CONFEDERATION OF SENEGAMBIA.

**SIERRA LEONE or
REPUBLIC OF SIERRA
LEONE**

Formerly the British •COLONY AND
PROTECTORATE OF SIERRA LEONE.
(The Colony proper included the
Sierra Leone peninsula and several
small islands; the interior regions
made up the Protectorate. However,
the Colony and Protectorate were
governed as a single overseas territory.) On April 27, 1961, SIERRA
LEONE became an independent state.
With a new constitution that became
effective in April, 1971, the country's
official name became REPUBLIC OF
SIERRA LEONE.

**SOCIALIST PEOPLE'S
LIBYAN ARAB
JAMAHIRIYA**

Current long-form name of LIBYA
(q.v.).

SOMALI DEMOCRATIC
REPUBLIC

See SOMALIA.

•SOMALI REPUBLIC

See SOMALIA.

SOMALIA or SOMALI
DEMOCRATIC REPUBLIC

Independent state in the Horn of
Africa established on July 1, 1960,
by the union of the •U.N. TRUST
TERRITORY OF SOMALILAND (under
Italian administration) and the pro-
tectorate of •BRITISH SOMALILAND
(Fig. 9). Known officially as the
•SOMALI REPUBLIC from 1960 through
1969; country then renamed SOMALI
DEMOCRATIC REPUBLIC following a
military coup.

Comment: The name SOMALIA has
been used with various meanings in
the period covered by this gazetteer.
Today, SOMALIA is the short-form
name for the SOMALI DEMOCRATIC
REPUBLIC. In the past, however,
the name SOMALIA was used popularly for the colony of •ITALIAN
SOMALILAND, and later for the U.N.
Trust Territory (1950-1960). (See
Supp. Notes III-A and III-D.)

•SOMALILAND, TRUST
TERRITORY OF (UNDER
ITALIAN ADMINISTRA-
TION)

See •ITALIAN SOMALILAND and
SOMALIA.

•SOMALILAND PROTEC-
TORATE or •BRITISH
SOMALILAND

British protectorate in the Horn of
Africa until 1960 (Fig. 9); continu-
ously under British administration
from the late 19th century except
for a brief period from August 1940
to March 1941 when it was occupied
by Italian forces (Fig. 11). The
protectorate was terminated on June
26, 1960; five days later the former
British dependency was united with
the •TRUST TERRITORY OF SOMALI-
LAND (the former •ITALIAN SOMALI-
LAND) to form the new •SOMALI

REPUBLIC (now the SOMALI DEMO-
CRATIC REPUBLIC). (See Supplementary Note III-C.)

•SOUDAN   See MALI.

•SOUDAN FRANÇAIS   See MALI.

•SOUDANAISE,●   See •SUDANESE REPUBLIC or MALI.
RÉPUBLIQUE

SOUTH AFRICA or   Formerly known as the •UNION OF
REPUBLIC OF SOUTH   SOUTH AFRICA. The Union, consti-
AFRICA   tuted May 31, 1910, by the unification
                                     of four British colonies, was a self-
                                     governing state with full Dominion
                                     Status under the British crown. In
                                     1920, the Union, on behalf of the
                                     League of Nations, assumed adminis-
                                     tration of the mandated territory of
                                     SOUTH WEST AFRICA (see Supp.
                                     Note I-E). Statutes enacted by the
                                     British (1931) and South African
                                     governments (1934) confirmed the
                                     sovereignty of the South African
                                     state, though it remained associated
                                     with the British Commonwealth of
                                     Nations. With the promulgation of a
                                     new constitution in May 1961, the
                                     country severed its ties with the
                                     Commonwealth and was renamed RE-
                                     PUBLIC OF SOUTH AFRICA.

                                     In recent years, the South African
                                     government ceded portions of its na-
                                     tional territory in ostensibly granting
                                     independence to the Black Homelands
                                     of TRANSKEI (1976), BOPHUTHA-
                                     TSWANA (1977), VENDA (1979), and
                                     CISKEI (1981) (Fig. 23). However,
                                     the international community has never
                                     recognized the sovereignty of those
                                     territories. (See Supp. Note VIII.)

                                     Comments: 1. South Africa con-
                                     tinues to administer SOUTH WEST
                                     AFRICA (now NAMIBIA [q.v.]), though

the U.N. advocates full independence for the territory.

2. WALVIS BAY (q.v.), a small zone along the coast of Namibia, is an enclave belonging to the Republic of South Africa (Fig. 1).

3. In 1947, South Africa took possession of two small islands (Prince Edward and Marion) in the southern Indian Ocean.

•SOUTH AFRICA,
UNION OF

See SOUTH AFRICA.

•SOUTH KASAI or
•MINING STATE

District of Kasai Province which seceded from the newly independent •REPUBLIC OF THE CONGO (now ZAIRE) in August, 1960 (Fig. 12). The short-lived secessionist state, also known as the •MINING STATE, appears to have again been fully integrated into the Congo state by 1962. See Supp. Note VII-A.

SOUTH WEST AFRICA (SWA) See NAMIBIA.

SOUTH WEST AFRICA /
NAMIBIA

See NAMIBIA.

•SOUTHERN (BRITISH)
CAMEROONS

See •BRITISH CAMEROONS or Supp. Note I-C.

•SOUTHERN MOROCCO,
(SPANISH) PROTEC-
TORATE OF

See •SPANISH SOUTHERN MOROCCO.

•SOUTHERN REGION
(OF SUDAN)

See SUDAN.

•SOUTHERN REGION (OF
THE UNITED ARAB
REPUBLIC)

See EGYPT.

•SOUTHERN RHODESIA   See ZIMBABWE or Supp. Note V-B.

Southern Sudan or   See SUDAN.
Southern Provinces of
Sudan

•SOUTHERN ZONE (OF   See SPANISH SOUTHERN MOROCCO
THE SPANISH PROTEC-   and Supp. Note IV-C.
TORATE IN MOROCCO)

•SPANISH EQUATORIAL   See EQUATORIAL GUINEA.
REGION

•SPANISH GUINEA   See EQUATORIAL GUINEA.

•SPANISH MOROCCO or   Former Spanish protectorate in north-
•SPANISH PROTECTOR-   western Africa; consisted of two non-
ATE IN MOROCCO   contiguous divisions separated by
                            •FRENCH MOROCCO (Fig. 20). The
                            •NORTHERN ZONE OF THE PROTEC-
                            TORATE, often shown as •SPANISH
                            MOROCCO or •SPANISH ZONE on
                            maps, was incorporated into the new
                            independent KINGDOM OF MOROCCO
                            in April 1956. The •SOUTHERN ZONE
                            OF THE PROTECTORATE (also known
                            as •SOUTHERN SPANISH MOROCCO
                            and by several other names) was
                            ceded to Morocco in 1958. (See Supp.
                            Note IV-A.)

                            Comment: The •INTERNATIONAL
                            ZONE OF TANGIER, which came under
                            Spanish control in 1940, was attached
                            to Spanish Morocco (Fig. 20). Tangier
                            was restored as an international zone
                            in 1945.

•SPANISH SAHARA   See WESTERN SAHARA.

Spanish North Africa   Term used for the small Spanish en-
                            claves of CEUTA and MELILLA and
                            several islands in the coastal regions
                            of MOROCCO. The areas are considered
                            part of metropolitan Spain.

•SPANISH SOUTHERN   Former Spanish-administered territory,
MOROCCO or •SOUTH-   officially the •SOUTHERN ZONE OF
ERN ZONE OF THE   THE SPANISH PROTECTORATE IN
SPANISH PROTEC-   MOROCCO (Fig. 20), though also
TORATE IN MOROCCO   identified by several names (viz.,
                           CAPE JUBY, •SOUTHERN MOROCCO,
                           •SOUTHERN PROTECTORATE [or
                           ZONE] OF SPANISH MOROCCO,
                           TARFAYA, •TEKNA, •ZONA AL SUR
                           DEL DRAA). The territory, which
                           had been administered as part of
                           •SPANISH WEST AFRICA for many
                           years, was finally ceded to MOROCCO
                           in 1958. (See Supp. Note IV-C.)

•SPANISH TERRITORIES   See EQUATORIAL GUINEA.
OF THE GULF OF
GUINEA

•SPANISH WEST AFRICA   Name adopted in 1946 for the newly
                           created Spanish overseas entity com-
                           prising the territories of •SPANISH
                           SAHARA (RÍO DE ORO and SAGUIA
                           EL HAMRA) and •IFNI; in addition the
                           protectorate of •SOUTHERN SPANISH
                           MOROCCO was integrated administra-
                           tively with Spanish Sahara (Fig. 20).
                           Spanish West Africa was dissolved in
                           1958 when Southern Spanish Morocco
                           was ceded to the KINGDOM OF MO-
                           ROCCO while Ifni and Spanish Sahara
                           were constituted provinces of the
                           Spanish state. Ifni was later ceded
                           to Morocco (1969). Spanish Sahara
                           (by then generally known as WEST-
                           ERN SAHARA) was partitioned in 1976
                           between MAURITANIA and the KING-
                           DOM OF MOROCCO.

                           Comment: For subsequent develop-
                           ments, refer to the entry on WESTERN
                           SAHARA and Supp. Note IV-C.

•SUD-KASAI   See •SOUTH KASAI.

SUDAN or REPUBLIC   From 1899 to the 1950's, the territory,
OF THE SUDAN   under the joint administration (condo-
                           minium) of the British and Egyptian

governments, was known as the
•ANGLO-EGYPTIAN SUDAN. The
two administering governments agreed
to grant the Sudanese greater autonomy, and a "transition government"
became operative during the period
1953-1956. Full independence was
granted January 1, 1956, the new
state officially becoming the REPUB-
LIC OF THE SUDAN. Following a
military coup in 1969, the long-form
name of the country became •DEMO-
CRATIC REPUBLIC OF THE SUDAN.
However, in December 1985, after
another coup, the denomination reverted to REPUBLIC OF THE SUDAN.

Comment: A genuine, effective
unification of the northern and southern regions in Sudan, Africa's largest
country, has yet to be achieved.
During the colonial period, the three
southern provinces, generally identified as •SOUTHERN SUDAN, were set
apart administratively within the
•ANGLO-EGYPTIAN SUDAN from 1930
to 1947. Following years of civil war
even after Sudan won its independence,
a 1972 agreement between the central
government and southern separatist
forces included autonomous status for
the southern provinces (Fig. 15); the
national constitution promulgated in
1973 formally recognized limited autonomy for the •SOUTHERN REGION.
A regional government was established
and given authority over internal affairs in southern Sudan. However,
the Southern Region was dissolved in
1983, and redivided into three administrative units.

SUDAN, REPUBLIC OF THE   See SUDAN.

•SUDANESE REPUBLIC   Name adopted by •FRENCH SUDAN
or •SOUDAN (RÉPUB-   when it became an autonomous member
LIQUE SOUDANAISE)   state in the French Community in 1958
                          (Fig. 19). The Sudanese Republic
                          briefly united with SENEGAL during

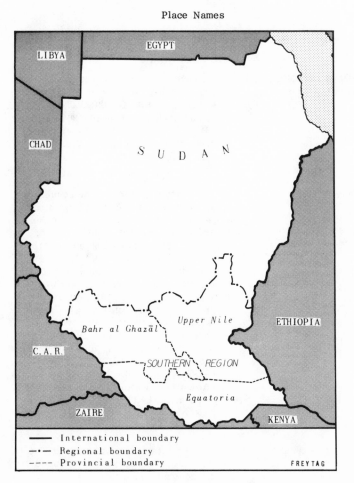

Fig. 15. The Southern Sudan.

1959-60 in the •FEDERATION OF MALI. Following dissolution of the Federation, the Sudanese Republic became the REPUBLIC OF MALI. (See Supp. Note II-B.)

Comment: Fortunately, the name •SUDANESE REPUBLIC, which could easily be confused with that of another country called REPUBLIC OF THE SUDAN, was used for only a short time.

SWA and SWA/NAMIBIA   See NAMIBIA.

SWAZILAND or KINGDOM   Formerly the British protectorate of
OF SWAZILAND   SWAZILAND, and one of the three
                             •HIGH COMMISSION TERRITORIES
                             of southern Africa until 1964 (Fig.
                             22). The kingdom became fully in-
                             dependent on September 6, 1968.
                             (See Supp. Note V-C.)

Tanganyika   The portion of the former colonial
                             territory of German East Africa which
                             became a mandated territory under
                             British administration after World
                             War I (Supp. Notes I-A and I-D).
                             The name •TANGANYIKA TERRITORY
                             was adopted for the mandate. The
                             mandate became a Trust Territory
                             under the U.N. in 1946, with the
                             United Kingdom continuing to serve
                             as the administrating authority.
                             TANGANYIKA achieved independence
                             on December 9, 1961, and one year
                             later became the •REPUBLIC OF
                             TANGANYIKA. In April, 1964,
                             TANGANYIKA joined with ZANZIBAR
                             to form the UNITED REPUBLIC OF
                             TANZANIA. (See TANZANIA and
                             Fig. 9.)

                             Comments: 1. After World War II,
                             the word "Territory" was dropped from
                             the conventional name.

                             2. Once the union of TANZANIA
                             had been consummated, the name
                             TANGANYIKA was still used in re-
                             ferring specifically to the mainland
                             portion of the new republic; now
                             MAINLAND TANZANIA is the accepted
                             name.

                             3. "Tanganyika" has not become
                             entirely an obsolete term, being the
                             name of a large African lake and one
                             still found in the titles of numerous
                             organizations on the mainland. Even
                             the name of the principal political
                             party of MAINLAND TANZANIA in-
                             cluded the word "Tanganyika" until 1977.

•TANGANYIKA,   See •TANGANYIKA and TANZANIA.
REPUBLIC OF

•TANGANYIKA AND   See TANZANIA.
ZANZIBAR, UNITED
REPUBLIC OF

•TANGANYIKA   See •TANGANYIKA.
TERRITORY

•TANGIER ZONE   Former enclave on the northern coast
[INTERNATIONAL   of MOROCCO (Fig. 20). Before
ZONE]   World War II, TANGIER ZONE was a
                         neutralized district under the control
                         of an international commission. In
                         1940, the international zone was an-
                         nexed by Spain. Spanish administra-
                         tion continued during the war, with
                         Tangier being incorporated into
                         •SPANISH MOROCCO. However, the
                         Spanish government agreed to a re-
                         sumption of international control of
                         the Tangier Zone in 1945.

                         Tangier was fully integrated (as a
                         province) into the independent KING-
                         DOM OF MOROCCO in October 1956.

                         Comment: Tangier has been re-
                         tained as the name of a city and prov-
                         ince in the Moroccan kingdom.

TANZANIA or UNITED   African nation created April 26, 1964,
REPUBLIC OF TANZANIA   by the union of the •REPUBLIC OF
                         TANGANYIKA on the African mainland
                         and the •PEOPLE'S REPUBLIC OF
                         ZANZIBAR (the islands of Zanzibar
                         and Pemba); both already were inde-
                         pendent countries (•TANGANYIKA
                         since December 9, 1961, and •ZANZI-
                         BAR from December 10, 1963). Though
                         first known as the "UNITED REPUBLIC
                         OF TANGANYIKA AND ZANZIBAR,
                         UNITED REPUBLIC OF TANZANIA
                         was adopted as the official name in
                         October 1964 (see Supp. Notes I-D
                         and VI-B, and Fig. 9).

Comment: The mainland of the
united republic, still mentioned as
•TANGANYIKA for several years
after the merger, is now referred to
as MAINLAND [TANZANIA].

Tanzania, Mainland   See Tanganyika and TANZANIA.

Tarfaya   One of the more frequently used
                            names for the former protectorate of
                            •SPANISH SOUTHERN MOROCCO (Fig.
                            20). The territory was ceded to
                            MOROCCO in 1958.

TCHAD   See CHAD.

•TEKNA [ZONE]   One of several variants for the former
                            protectorate of •SPANISH SOUTHERN
                            MOROCCO, a territory that became
                            part of the KINGDOM OF MOROCCO
                            in 1958.

•TERRITOIRE DES   See COMORO ISLANDS.
COMORES

•TERRITOIRE FRANÇAIS   See DJIBOUTI.
DES AFARS ET DES
ISSAS or T.F.A.I.

•T.F.A.I.   See DJIBOUTI.

THE GAMBIA   See GAMBIA.

TOGO; officially REPUBLIC   Formerly the French-administered
OF TOGO or TOGOLESE   Trust Territory (previously a man-
REPUBLIC (RÉPUBLIQUE   date) of •FRENCH TOGO[LAND];
TOGOLAISE)   after 1946 formally referred to as
                            the •TRUST TERRITORY OF TOGO-
                            LAND UNDER FRENCH ADMINISTRA-
                            TION, yet considered an "Associated
                            Territory" of the French Union (see
                            Supp. Notes I-A and I-B).

French Togoland was declared a
self-governing "Autonomous Republic"
in 1956 by the French government,
but the U.N. continued to treat it as
a Trust Territory (Fig. 3). The
trusteeship of •FRENCH TOGO was
eventually terminated, with the
REPUBLIC OF TOGO gaining full
independence on April 27, 1960.

Comment: The name TOGO or
TOGOLAND was also used collectively
for British and French Togo[land].

•TOGO, AUTONOMOUS   See Supp. Note I-B.
REPUBLIC OF

TOGOLAISE, RÉPUBLIQUE   See TOGO.

TRANSKEI or REPUBLIC   Formerly one of several autonomous
OF TRANSKEI   "Black (or Tribal) Homelands" es-
                           tablished within the REPUBLIC OF
                           SOUTH AFRICA (Fig. 23). Granted
                           independence as a self-governing
                           republic by the South African govern-
                           ment on October 26, 1976. However,
                           Transkei's sovereignty has been rec-
                           ognized only by South Africa, but by
                           neither any other country nor by the
                           United Nations. (See Supp. Note
                           VIII.)

                           Comment: TRANSKEI was the
                           first of the South African "Homelands"
                           to accept full independence.

Tripolitania   See CYRENAICA, TRIPOLITANIA,
                           and FEZZAN; also see Supp. Note
                           III-B.

•TRUST TERRITORY   See •RUANDA-URUNDI.
OF RUANDA-URUNDI

•TRUST TERRITORY OF SOMALILAND (UNDER ITALIAN ADMINISTRA- TION

See •ITALIAN SOMALILAND or Supp. Note III-D.

•TRUST TERRITORY OF TOGOLAND UNDER BRITISH ADMINISTRA- TION

See •BRITISH TOGO[LAND].

•TRUST TERRITORY OF TOGOLAND UNDER FRENCH ADMINISTRA- TION

See TOGO.

TUNIS

See TUNISIA.

TUNISIA or REPUBLIC OF TUNISIA (TUNISIE)

Formerly a French protectorate in North Africa. Administered by the collaborationist Vichy government after the fall of France in 1940; territory became a battleground in the North African campaign from November 1942 until May 1943. Following withdrawal by the Axis forces, control of Tunisia was assumed by the Free French until the French Republic was restored af- ter the war.

TUNISIA achieved full independence as a constitutional monarchy on March 20, 1956. When the monarchy was abolished in July, 1957, the REPUBLIC OF TUNISIA was formally proclaimed.

Comment: TUNIS, the name of the largest city, is also a variant name for the entire country.

TUNISIE

French spelling of TUNISIA (q.v.).

•U.A.R.

See EGYPT.

•UBANGI-SHARI

See CENTRAL AFRICAN REPUBLIC.

UGANDA or REPUBLIC   Formerly •UGANDA PROTECTORATE,
OF UGANDA   a British dependency within the realm
                            popularly known as •BRITISH EAST
                            AFRICA in the colonial period.
                            UGANDA achieved independence on
                            October 9, 1962. With the adoption
                            of a new constitution in 1967, the
                            country was proclaimed the REPUBLIC
                            OF UGANDA.

•UGANDA PROTEC-   See UGANDA.
 TORATE

•UNION OF SOUTH   See SOUTH AFRICA.
 AFRICA

•UNITED ARAB RE-   See EGYPT.
 PUBLIC (U.A.R.)

•UNITED REPUBLIC   See CAMEROON.
 OF CAMEROON

•UNITED REPUBLIC   See TANZANIA.
 OF TANGANYIKA
 AND ZANZIBAR

UNITED REPUBLIC OF   See TANZANIA.
TANZANIA

•UPPER IVORY COAST   See IVORY COAST or BURKINA.

•UPPER VOLTA or   See BURKINA.
 •REPUBLIC OF
 UPPER VOLTA

•URUNDI   See BURUNDI.

VENDA or REPUBLIC   Formerly one of several autonomous
OF VENDA   "Black (or Tribal) Homelands" estab-
                            lished within the REPUBLIC OF
                            SOUTH AFRICA (Fig. 23). Granted

full independence by the South African government on September 13, 1979.

Venda's sovereign status is recognized only by South Africa, but by no other major states of the international community; it has not been invited to membership in the United Nations. (See Supp. Note VIII.)

•VOLTAIC (or •VOLTA)   See BURKINA.
REPUBLIC

•VOLTAÏQUE,   See BURKINA.
RÉPUBLIQUE

Walvis Bay   Small political division along the coast of NAMIBIA (SOUTH WEST AFRICA). (Refer to Fig. 1 for location.) Though legally an exclave of SOUTH AFRICA'S Cape Province, Walvis Bay was administratively attached to the mandate of South West Africa from 1922 to 1977. Walvis Bay has since been under direct jurisdiction of Cape Province. (See Supp. Note I-E.)

•WEST CAMEROON   See CAMEROON.

Western Sahara   Political division of northwestern Africa known as •SPANISH SAHARA from the 1930s until the mid-1970s, and which currently is a disputed territory.

By the mid-1930s, the Spanish were strengthening political and military control over their possessions along the northwestern coast of Africa, viz., RÍO DE ORO and SAGUIA EL HAMRA (two districts often referred to as "Spanish [Western] Sahara"), plus the small coastal colony of •IFNI (Fig. 20). Administrative responsibility for those territories was assigned to the government of the

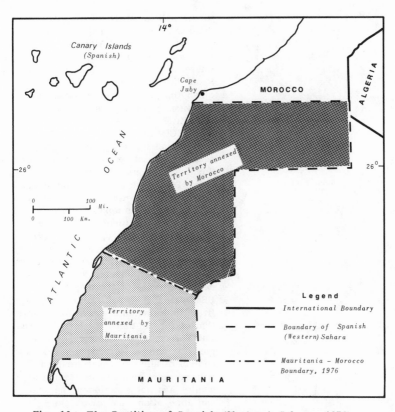

Fig. 16.   The Partition of Spanish (Western) Sahara, 1976.
(Since 1979, Moroccan forces have occupied the
entire Western Saharan territory.)

•SPANISH PROTECTORATE IN
MOROCCO. In 1946, the ties of
•SPANISH SAHARA and •IFNI with
the protectorate were severed, and
the two territories consolidated as
the overseas entity called •SPANISH
WEST AFRICA. •SOUTHERN SPANISH
MOROCCO, though technically the
southern zone of the Spanish Protectorate, was integrated for administrative purposes with Spanish Sahara
and therefore also considered part of
Spanish West Africa. Spanish West
Africa was dissolved in 1958 when
Southern Spanish Morocco was ceded

to the KINGDOM OF MOROCCO, while
Spanish Sahara (formally designated
the PROVINCE OF SAHARA) and Ifni
were made Spanish provinces. Ifni
was ceded to Morocco in 1969, and
Spain finally agreed in 1975 to relinquish the province of Spanish Sahara
(by then generally referred to as
WESTERN SAHARA). In 1976,
MOROCCO and MAURITANIA decided
to partition Western Sahara, with
each incorporating part of the former
Spanish area into its national territory
(Fig. 16). The partition, however,
was opposed by the Polisario Front,
an indigenous nationalist group striv-
ing to gain full independence for the
Western Saharan peoples. Following
Spanish withdrawal from the territory
in early 1976, the Polisario Front pro-
calimed the establishment of a government (in-exile) of the SAHARAN
DEMOCRATIC ARAB REPUBLIC (SADR).
In 1979, Mauritania ended its occupation of the southern Western Sahara,
but Moroccan forces immediately occupied the zone. Morocco now claims
control of all the former Western
Sahara. Yet the international community has not sanctioned the Moroccan annexation; moreover, the Polisario Front is now recognized and
supported by a number of nations.
By late 1986, the status of Western
Sahara was yet to be resolved. (See
Supp. Note IV-C.)

ZAIRE or REPUBLIC
OF ZAIRE

Formerly the colony of •BELGIAN
CONGO. From 1925 to 1960, the
Belgian mandate (late Trust Terri-
tory) of •RUANDA-URUNDI was also
affiliated with the colony (see Supp.
Note I-D). The Belgian Congo was
granted full independence on June 30,
1960, becoming •REPUBLIC OF THE
CONGO (•RÉPUBLIQUE DU CONGO).
(Ruanda-Urundi remained a Belgian
Trust Territory until 1962.) In July
1960, the southern province of
•KATANGA seceded, and in August,

the •MINING STATE OF SOUTH KASAI
also proclaimed its independence (Fig.
12). By early 1963, both were again
incorporated into the Congo state.
(See Supp. Notes VII-A and VII-B.)
With the promulgation of a new constitution in August 1964, the country's
long-form name became •DEMOCRATIC
REPUBLIC OF THE CONGO. In October 1971, REPUBLIC OF ZAIRE was
adopted as the official name for the
state.

Comment: The French territory of
•MIDDLE CONGO and the •BELGIAN
CONGO became independent countries
in 1960. Each also chose •RÉPUBLIQUE
DU CONGO (French was the official
language in both countries) as its new
name; CONGO was the short-form name
for both. To clearly differentiate the
two countries, it became customary,
following a precedent established in
the United Nations, to add the name
of the capital city to both the long-
and short-form names. Thus, the
former Belgian Congo was referred to
as •REPUBLIC OF THE CONGO (LEO-
POLDVILLE) or •CONGO-LEOPOLDVILLE
from 1960 to 1966; when the capital
was renamed, the short-form became
•CONGO-KINSHASA. (The former
French area was known as •REPUBLIC
OF CONGO [BRAZZAVILLE] or
•CONGO-BRAZZAVILLE). The confusion ended in 1971 when ZAIRE was
adopted as the name for Congo-
Kinshasa.

ZAMBIA or REPUBLIC
OF ZAMBIA

Formerly the British protectorate of
•NORTHERN RHODESIA, which included the territory of BAROTSELAND
(q.v.). From 1953 to 1963, •NORTH-
ERN RHODESIA was one of three British areas included in the •FEDERATION
OF RHODESIA AND NYASALAND.
Following the dissolution of the federation, •NORTHERN RHODESIA remained briefly under British administration prior to being granted

independence on October 24, 1964.
ZAMBIA was adopted as the name for
the new republic. (See Fig. 21.)

Zanzibar

Former offshore British protectorate
comprising the islands of Zanzibar
and Pemba (Fig. 9).

ZANZIBAR became independent
December 10, 1963, but after the
sultanate was overthrown in January
1964, the political unit was renamed
•PEOPLE'S REPUBLIC OF ZANZIBAR.
In April 1964, ZANZIBAR merged with
the •REPUBLIC OF TANGANYIKA
forming the •UNITED REPUBLIC OF
TANGANYIKA AND ZANZIBAR (now
UNITED REPUBLIC OF TANZANIA).
(See Supp. Note VI-B.)

Comments: 1. The Sultan of
Zanzibar's domain also included a
coastal strip on the mainland [the
•KENYA PROTECTORATE] that was
administered by the British as part
of •KENYA COLONY. However, the
coastal protectorate was ceded to the
new Kenyan state in 1963.

2. The name ZANZIBAR, long
applied to the archipelago as a whole,
is also the toponym of the principal
island and the largest city.

•ZANZIBAR, PEOPLE'S
REPUBLIC OF

See ZANZIBAR and TANZANIA.

ZIMBABWE or REPUBLIC
OF ZIMBABWE

Formerly the British self-governing
colony of •SOUTHERN RHODESIA;
joined with two other British dependencies in 1953 to form the •FEDERA-
TION OF RHODESIA AND NYASALAND
(Fig. 21). Following dissolution of
the federation in 1963, the colony's
name was shortened to •RHODESIA
(1964). In November 1965, Rhodesia
declared its independence, but Rhodesian sovereignty was never formally

recognized either by Britain or any other country. The government in February 1970 announced that Rhodesia, under its new constitution, had become a republic.

In June 1979, as a result of meetings between white and black leaders, a new government was formed and the country's name changed to •ZIMBABWE RHODESIA. Yet the new arrangement was considered unacceptable, leading to further conferences under British sponsorship. The parliament of Zimbabwe Rhodesia was dissolved in December 1979, the territory then reverting to British control; officially, the name •SOUTHERN RHODESIA was again adopted for a short time. Following elections and the establishment of a new government, the REPUBLIC OF ZIMBABWE was declared independent on April 18, 1980. Its government was also acknowledged to be a legally constituted body entitled to formal recognition by the international community of nations. (See Supp. Note V-B.)

•ZIMBABWE RHODESIA   See ZIMBABWE or Supp. Note V-B.

•ZONA AL SUR DEL   See •SPANISH SOUTHERN MOROCCO.
DRAA

PART THREE: SUPPLEMENTARY
NOTES AND MAPS

This section provides additional information on particular African regions and states. The supplementary notes which follow, not deemed either essential or appropriate for inclusion with the entries in the gazetteer, may be of interest and a possible aid to some users.

The reader should not misconstrue the author's intent in preparing these supplementary notes and maps. Cumulatively, these materials represent but a modest augmentation of the gazetteer (Part Two). Thus, the reader should not expect to find here a handy capsulization or record of major political events throughout Africa during the past half-century. Anyone seeking a fuller explanation and interpretation of those complex political developments is directed to a number of excellent works listed in the selected bibliography (Part Four).

I. AFRICAN TERRITORIES WITH SPECIAL STATUS:
MANDATES AND TRUSTEESHIPS

A. Introduction

By 1935, all of Africa had been partitioned into numerous political territories, most of which were colonies or protectorates. Seven territories, however, were not traditional dependencies, having acquired special status as mandated areas.

The assignment of mandatory powers after World War I represented a new approach for the governance of dependencies

which were relinquished by a defeated nation. When the
Germans signed the Treaty of Versailles, they renounced
claims to their onetime African territories of Togo, Kamerun
(Cameroon), German East Africa, and German South West
Africa. Those four areas, already occupied by Allied forces
before the war ended, eventually were placed under the general supervision of the League of Nations, the multinational
political body established in 1920. The League in turn
granted mandates to established governments which were to
assume reponsibility for administering the former German
possessions. With three of those German territories also
partitioned, the appearance of seven mandated areas neces-
sitated several corrections on the political map of Africa by
the early 1920s (Table 1 and Fig. 17).

Table 1:

MANDATED TERRITORIES OF AFRICA
ESTABLISHED AFTER WORLD WAR I

German Colony	Mandated Territories	Mandatory Power
German East Africa	Tanganyika Territory	Britain
	Ruanda-Urundi	Belgium
German South West Africa	South West Africa	Union of South Africa*
Kamerun	British Cameroons	Britain
	French Cameroon(s)	France
Togo	British Togoland	Britain
	French Togoland	France

*Now the Republic of South Africa.

The mandatory powers were accountable to the League's
Permanent Mandates Commission. In practice, however, the

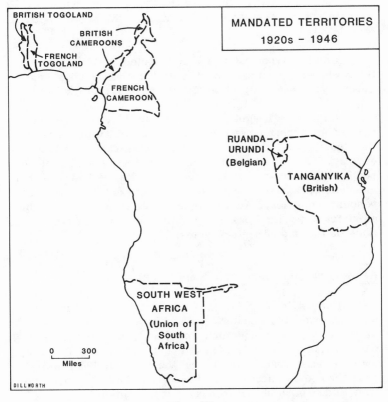

Fig. 17.

mandated areas were administered much as other overseas
dependencies held by the mandatory powers. In some instances, the mandates became administrative extensions of
existing colonies, e.g., Ruanda-Urundi was governed essentially by the Belgians as a province of the Belgian Congo.

The League of Nations was formally dissolved in 1946,
and superseded by the United Nations (U.N.) as an international political organization. General supervision for the
mandated territories was transferred from the defunct League
to the U.N., one of whose special agencies was a Trusteeship
Council to oversee the administration of the former mandates,
now to be called Trust Territories. All the mandatory powers
except South Africa signed trusteeship agreements, in effect
confirming transfer of general authority for the delegated

mandates to the U.N. Only South Africa refused to place its
mandate (South West Africa) under the U.N. (See Supp.
Note I-E.)

Another trusteeship was constituted in 1950 when the
U.N. made the onetime colony of Italian Somaliland a Trust
Territory. (See Supp. Note III-D and Fig. 9.)

Unlike the League of Nations, the U.N. emphasized
that administering powers had a responsibility to prepare
the Trust Territories for eventual independence. Consequently, by 1962 all the trusteeship agreements in Africa
had been terminated as the various territories had achieved
independent status outright or were annexed to other independent countries. Additional background on the individual
mandates/trust territories is provided in this and other sections of the supplementary notes.

B.   British and French Togoland

Germany's West African colony of Togo was divided
into two mandated territories. The eastern portion of the
former colony became French Togo[land] and the western
part British Togo[land] (Table 1 and Fig. 17). Both mandates became trusteeships under the U.N. in 1946, and
from then known formally as the "Trust Territory of Togoland Under (British or French) Administration."

Although British Togo was considered by the British
to be an integral administrative division of their adjoining
colony of Gold Coast, within the French system, French
Togoland was regarded a special dependency rather than a
colony. Thus, under the new French constitution in 1946,
French Togo was classified an "Associated Territory" within
the colonial federation of French West Africa. This was a
subtle but not insignificant distinction from other French
dependencies categorized as "Overseas Territories" within
the French Republic.

A U.N.-supervised plebiscite was conducted in British
Togoland in 1956. Following the African peoples' wishes expressed by their votes, the trusteeship status was terminated
by the U.N. in 1957 allowing British Togoland to unite with
the Gold Coast to form the independent state of Ghana (Fig. 3).

The French authorities conducted their own plebiscite in French Togoland in 1956, offering the African population an opportunity to terminate the trusteeship. The vote supported the French proposal, and was followed by the proclamation of the establishment of an "Autonomous Republic of Togo." The U.N., which had neither sanctioned the referendum nor approved the unilateral action taken by the French government, continued to regard French Togoland as a Trust Territory until 1960. When the trusteeship status was formally terminated by the U.N. in 1960, the independent Republic of Togo came into existence.

C. The Cameroons

The onetime German colony of Kamerun was partitioned by the League of Nations into the mandated territories of French Cameroon(s) and British Cameroon(s) (Fig. 17 and Table 1). In 1946 the two areas, then assigned as trusteeships under the United Nations, were formally designated the "Cameroons under French Administration" and the "[Territory of the] Cameroons under British Administration." French Cameroon, administered by the French as a special territorial unit, was granted full independence in 1960 as the Republic of Cameroon (Cameroun).

The British Cameroons consisted of the Northern and Southern Cameroons (Fig. 3). The divisions were attached for administrative convenience to the neighboring British colony of Nigeria: Northern Cameroons was considered part of Nigeria's Northern Provinces (or Northern Region after 1939); Southern Cameroons was under the government of the Southern Provinces (Eastern Region from 1939). In 1954, the Trust Territory of Southern Cameroons was given status equivalent to that of a provincial division within the Nigerian federation. Before Nigeria became independent, however, the whole of the British trusteeship ceased to be politically affiliated with the Nigerian state.

In February 1961, the U.N. conducted a plebiscite in the Northern and Southern Cameroons to decide whether the territories would be merged with Nigeria or Cameroon. Following the people's preferences expressed in the plebescite, Northern Cameroons was incorporated into Nigeria in June, and Southern Cameroons federated with Cameroon in October.

With the British Cameroons having thereby been dissolved
with U.N. approval, the trust territory was replaced by a
new common boundary for Nigeria and Cameroon (Fig. 3).

The Southern (British) Cameroons merger with the
Republic of Cameroon accomplished, a political entity known
as the Federal Republic of Cameroon was established (Fig.
5). The new federal republic consisted of two autonomous
states: East Cameroon (the onetime French Cameroon [Re-
public of Cameroon in 1960-61]) and West Cameroon (the
former Southern Cameroons). Revisions of the Cameroonian
constitution in 1972 led to the replacement of the federal
structure by a unitary government. Consequently, the
federated states of East and West Cameroon were abolished,
and the country divided into seven provinces. These
changes in the country's internal political structure also
resulted in the country being renamed United Republic of
Cameroon. However, recent constitutional revisions (1984)
again made Republic of Cameroon the official name.

D. Tanganyika and Ruanda-Urundi

The onetime protectorate of German East Africa was
partitioned into two mandated areas after World War I (Table
1 and Fig. 17). Though two districts (Ruanda-Urundi) were
assigned to the Belgians, the greater part of the area was
designated a British-administered mandate known as Tanganyika
Territory.

1. Tanganyika and Tanzania. In 1920, the British
began using the name Tanganyika Territory for the mandated area entrusted to them. Following World War II,
Tanganyika became a U.N. Trust Territory, with Britain
continuing as the administering authority. The word "Territory" was dropped from the conventional name, however.
The trusteeship was terminated in 1961, and Tanganyika
awarded full independence. With revisions made in the
constitution a year later, the country officially became the
Republic of Tanganyika.

In April 1964, the Republic of Tanganyika and the offshore People's Republic of Zanzibar merged to form what first
was called the United Republic of Tanganyika and Zanzibar,
but renamed United Republic of Tanzania later in the year.

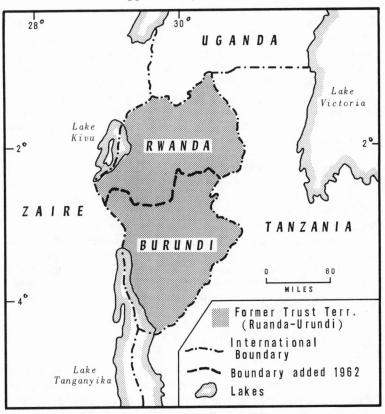

Fig. 18.   Rwanda and Burundi (formerly
Ruanda-Urundi).

Although the mainland division was still called Tanganyika
after 1964, Mainland Tanzania is now the preferred denomination.

An interim constitution for the united republic was
drawn up in 1965. But in 1977 President Nyerere announced
establishment of a single national party to supersede the two
existing political organizations, one of which had been domi-
nant in Mainland Tanzania and the other in Zanzibar. Though
the new constitution was expected to solidify the union, the
government in Zanzibar retains considerable jurisdiction in
many local matters.

2. <u>From Ruanda-Urundi to Rwanda and Burundi</u>. Until
World War I, Ruanda and Urundi were districts in the northwestern area of German East Africa. Following the war they
were consolidated as the Belgian-administered mandate of
Ruanda-Urundi (Fig. 17). In 1925 the mandated territory
was administratively joined with the Belgian Congo. That
arrangement continued after the dissolution of the League of
Nations in 1946, Ruanda-Urundi remaining under Belgian administration as a U.N. Trust Territory.

In 1960, as the Belgian Congo celebrated its independence, separate preparations were underway for the upcoming
independence of the Trust Territory previously attached to
the colony. The U.N. proposed to create a federal state,
but differences between peoples of the northern (Ruanda)
and southern (Urundi) divisions proved irreconcilable. The
U.N. finally acceded to demands of local African leaders to
create two sovereign nations (Fig. 18). In 1962, the trusteeship was terminated, Ruanda-Urundi divided, and independence awarded to the countries called Rwanda and Burundi.

E. Namibia (South West Africa)

The most publicized and controversial of the mandated
areas is the former German protectorate of South West Africa.
Following World War I, the League of Nations conferred to
"his Britannic Majesty" a mandate for administering the former German territory (Fig. 17 and Table 1). That mandate,
however, was to be exercised by the Union of South Africa,
then a British dominion, on behalf of Britain. Walvis Bay,
a coastal exclave legally part of South Africa's Cape Province
(Fig. 1), was administratively attached to the mandate in
1922.

During the inter-war period, South Africa was accorded
recognition as an independent state as were other British
dominions; dominions were even admitted to full membership
in the League. The South African authorities, though accountable to the League respecting their governance of South
West Africa, were permitted to treat it as an integral division
of their national state.

The mandate for South West Africa continued through
the end of World War II. But after the League of Nations was

dissolved in 1946, South Africa's leaders decided they had neither the obligation nor any intention of transferring general supervision for South West Africa to the Trusteeship Council of the United Nations. The South Africans, finding no support in the U.N. for their proposal to totally annex South West Africa, announced they would continue administering the territory in the "spirit" of the defunct League's original mandate rather than complying with a trusteeship agreement.

Despite the passage of numerous resolutions and other actions taken by the U.N. on the issue of South West Africa, the South Africans steadfastly refused to relinquish their "mandate." After years of unsuccessful attempts to negotiate a settlement, the U.N. passed a resolution in 1966, this time formally terminating the mandate; continuation of South African rule thus was presumed to constitute illegal occupation of South West Africa. A special U.N. council even was created with responsibility for administration of the territory, which, it was hoped, would soon join the ranks of independent states. Nevertheless, all such resolutions were ignored, the South Africans averring the U.N. never had the legal authority to terminate the mandate.

Since the late 1940s, then, the status of South West Africa has been a recurrent issue at the U.N. The U.N. even adopted Namibia as the name for the territory. Yet in the mid-1970s the South African government had begun calling conferences to discuss the future of Namibia. The international community has been anxious for a peaceful settlement, but disagreements on specific points continue to delay Namibia's oft-announced independence. Walvis Bay, for example, again came directly under the jurisdiction of Cape Province in 1977. Namibian nationalists, on the other hand, want the South Africans to cede the diminutive coastal zone which could then be totally integrated into the national territory of an independent Namibia.

At this time, Namibia remains the only sizable political territory of Africa which is not a sovereign state.

II. THE FRENCH COLONIAL FEDERATIONS IN WEST AND EQUATORIAL AFRICA

A. Introduction

There were, until 1958, two major federations of French territories in Africa (Fig. 19): French West Africa (Afrique Occidentale Française) and French Equatorial Africa (Afrique Equatoriale Française). After World War II, the new constitution of the Fourth French Republic gave birth to the French Union. The two overseas federations, each with a centralized administration, retained essentially the same organizational framework that prevailed in the pre-war French Empire. However, the separate "colonies" making up the federations were designated "Overseas Territories" within the French Union. While African peoples gained some political rights, French officials still held considerable authority in the overseas areas.

After the war, the mandated territories of French Togo and French Cameroons remained under French administration, but as U.N. Trust Territories. They were classified as "Associated Territories" within the French Union (see Supp. Notes I-B and I-C).

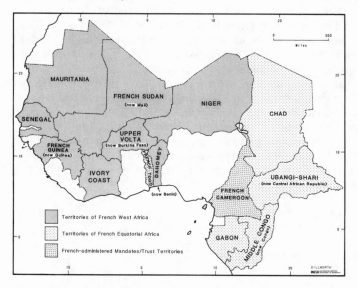

Fig. 19. French West Africa and French Equatorial Africa.

By the mid-1950s, the centralized political and economic power of the federations began to weaken as governments in each of the Overseas Territories were beginning to assume increasing responsibility for internal matters. In part, this was a result of reforms introduced in 1956 and 1957 calling for greater self-government in the territories. Even the constitution proposed by President de Gaulle in 1958 contained provisions for a new organizational structure involving France and its overseas dependencies.

In September, 1958, a referendum on the new constitution was held in each territory. Those territories approving the constitution were to become participating members of de Gaulle's newly-structured French Community that was to supersede the French Union. All but one of the twelve territories in the two federations approved the new constitution and thus accepted an autonomous (but non-sovereign) member-states of the Community. French Guinea, the single territory rejecting the constitution, was granted full independence immediately (October 1958) and proclaimed the Republic of Guinea.

During 1959, the territories were clearly being transformed into self-governing entities. The federal bodies for French West Africa and French Equatorial Africa, virtually ineffective by then, were dissolved quietly. Yet the grand plan for an integrated Community of francophone territories was never to be realized because all of the "autonomous" units succeeded in achieving full independence in 1960. (At the time, Senegal and the Sudanese Republic [now Mali] were united in the short-lived Mali Federation.)

B. French West Africa

By the late 1930s, French West Africa, the larger of the federations, included the seven colonies of Dahomey, French Guinea, French Sudan, Ivory Coast, Mauritania, Niger, and Senegal (including the special District of Dakar). The entire federation was administered by a Governor-General, though each of the colonies had its own Governor (Lieutenant-Governor until 1937). The mandated territory of French Togo, technically not an administrative unit within the federation, was often regarded as part of it. From 1940 to 1942, French West Africa had a pro-Vichy administration,

but came under Free French authority for the remainder of
the war period.

The seven "Overseas Territories" became eight in 1947
when Upper Volta, a colony dissolved in 1932, was reconstituted (Fig. 19). The lands of Upper Volta, previously divided among the colonies of Ivory Coast, Niger, and French
Sudan, were conjoined in reviving the separate unit (Fig. 4).

In 1958, seven of the territories opted to continue
their affiliation with France, but as autonomous divisions of
the new French Community. Those territories also adopted
new official names at that time:

Name of Overseas Territory (until 1958)	Name Adopted as Member State of French Community (1958)
Dahomey	Republic of Dahomey (now Benin)
French Sudan	Sudanese Republic (now Mali)
Ivory Coast	Republic of the Ivory Coast
Mauritania	Islamic Republic of Mauritania
Niger	Republic of Niger
Senegal	Republic of Senegal
Upper Volta	Voltaic Republic, then Republic of Upper Volta (now Burkina Faso)

In January 1959, four of the autonomous states of the
Community--Sudanese Republic, Senegal, Dahomey, and Upper Volta--agreed to join together as the Federation of Mali.
(Mali had been the name of a Sudanic empire in the medieval
period.) Dahomey and Upper Volta shortly reversed their
decisions to participate in the proposed union; therefore, the
Federation of Mali formally established in April consisted only
of Senegal and the Sudanese Republic. On June 20, 1960,
the federation became a fully independent state. However,
on August 20, the Senegalese withdrew from the federation;
a month later, the Sudanese Republic conceded that the federation was dead. Each territory thereafter was recognized
as a sovereign state, the Republic of Senegal retaining its
former name, but the Sudanese Republic renamed Republic
of Mali.

C. French Equatorial Africa

Until 1934, French Equatorial Africa was a federation comprising the colonies of Chad, Gabon, Middle Congo, and Ubangi-Shari (Fig. 19). French Cameroon, though technically a mandate, was considered an affiliated unit of the federation. Hoping to achieve greater efficiency and economies, the French Government reconstituted the federation into a single colony in 1934, and the four political divisions then designated regions. However, as various schemes to restructure French Equatorial Africa proved unwieldy, by the end of 1937 a federal system was again operative.

After the French government signed an armistice with Nazi Germany in 1940, officials in French Equatorial Africa acted to recognize the authority of the Free French government of General Charles de Gaulle. Free French forces and supporters took over the administration of the territories, and Brazzaville (the administrative capital for French Equatorial Africa) became the headquarters of the High Commission of Free French Africa.

The four Overseas Territories of the post-war federation became autonomous member-states of the French Community in 1958. As in French West Africa, the change in status was reflected in the adoption of new official names:

Name of Overseas Territory (until 1958)	Official Name Adopted 1958
Chad	Republic of Chad
Gabon	Gabonese Republic
Middle Congo	Republic of Congo (now People's Republic of the Congo)
Ubangi-Shari	Central African Republic

III. THE FORMER ITALIAN COLONIAL TERRITORIES OF AFRICA, 1935-1952

A. Introduction

By 1935, Italy held three colonies on the African

mainland: Libya in northern Africa, and Eritrea and Italian
Somaliland in eastern Africa (Figs. 11 and 13). Italy then enlarged its empire through the invasion and conquest of Ethiopia in 1935-36. Yet by the early 1940s, unsuccessful in its
defense against allied forces, Italy had lost its African colonies. However, the future status of those territories, apart
from Ethiopia whose sovereignty was restored in 1941, was
unresolved for a number of years. The disposition of the
former colonies of Libya, Italian Somaliland, and Eritrea ultimately had to be decided by the new United Nations organization during the late 1940s and early 1950s. This resulted
in two territories (Libya, Italian Somaliland) gaining independence, and the third (Eritrea) being federated with the Ethiopian empire.

B. Libya

After 1912, the northern African territory of Libya
(Libia), comprising the historical regions of Cyrenaica,
Tripolitania, and Fezzan, was an Italian dependency. However, Tripolitania and Cyrenaica were not formally consolidated into the colony of Libya (also referred to as Italian
Libia) until 1934; the southern region (Fezzan) continued to
be administered as a military zone. The provinces of northern Libya were fully incorporated into the Italian state in
1939 (Fig. 13).

By early 1943, Italian forces had been driven from
Libya. For some years thereafter, the territory was not administered as a single entity. The regions of Cyrenaica and
Tripolitania were each placed under control of British military
administrative units, while most of Fezzan came under French
control (Fig. 13). Despite the division into three administrative zones which continued through the 1940s, maps and
standard references published at the time generally continued
to portray Libya as a single political entity.

Numerous proposals on Libya's future were presented
at the United Nations. Finally, it was agreed that the three
divisions should be reunited as a federal state. In December,
1951, the United Kingdom of Libya was proclaimed--the first
country to be directly granted independence by the U.N.

The Libyan state remained a constitutional monarchy

with a federal structure until the early 1960s. The federal
system was then abolished, and the three provinces replaced
by ten new internal divisions; as a result, the word "United"
was expunged from the long-form name which in 1963 became
simply the Kingdom of Libya. Following the overthrow of the
monarchy by a military coup in 1969, the country was renamed
Libyan Arab Republic. In 1977, the government approved
modifications in the political structure; those changes were
evidenced in the adoption of Socialist People's Libyan Arab
Jamahiriya as the new official name.

C. Italian East Africa: 1936-41

        In October, 1935, Italian forces invaded Ethiopia and
completed their conquest in May, 1936. The Italians then
decided to amalgamate Ethiopia with their older colonies of
Eritrea and Italian Somaliland, thereby creating an Italian
Empire of East Africa, or Italian East Africa (Fig. 11). The
newly formed overseas entity was divided into five principal
provinces; the city of Addis Ababa and vicinity constituted
an additional special district. Two of the provinces were the
former colonial territories of Eritrea and (Italian) Somaliland,
both substantially enlarged in area by boundaries drawn for
the new provinces making up Italian East Africa. The Italians
would also capture and hold British Somaliland from August,
1940 until March, 1941, a brief period when Italian domination
was almost complete in the "Horn" of eastern Africa.

        In the early part of World War II, the Italians were
forced to withdraw from eastern Africa, and Italian East Africa was dissolved by the end of 1941. The monarchy and
sovereignty of the Ethiopian state were restored while British
Somaliland again became a protectorate.

        Having expelled the Italians, the British proceeded to
occupy those regions which, until 1936, had been the colonies
of Eritrea and Italian Somaliland. The enlarged (Italian)
Somaliland province of Italian East Africa included the Ogaden,
a region which had been part of Ethiopia's national territory
before 1936 (Figs. 9 and 11). Thus, it was an enlarged
Somaliland which fell under British jurisdiction, and the restored Ethiopian government contested British assumption of
control in the Ogaden region. The matter was ultimately decided in favor of the Ethiopian crown which resumed

administration of Ogaden and other areas recognized as having been part of the Ethiopian state before the Italian period
of occupation.

D. The Status of Italian Somaliland and Eritrea After 1941

The future of Eritrea and Italian Somaliland, like that
of Libya, ultimately had to be resolved by the United Nations
in the post-war period (Fig. 9). Through the late 1940s,
numerous proposals were offered by members of the U.N.
concerning the future of the onetime Italian colonies still under British military administration. Eventually each territory
was granted status that seemed appropriate to its particular
circumstances.

The former Italian Somaliland remained under the British until 1950 when the U.N. designated it a Trust Territory
whose administration was to be entrusted to the Italian government for ten years (also see Supp. Note I-A). During
that period of tutelage (1950-1960), the "Territory of Somaliland under Italian Administration," as it was known formally,
was to undergo preparation for self-government. The territory would often be referred to by the old name "Italian
Somaliland" or simply as "Somalia," though, of course, it
was no longer an Italian "colony." Following the timetable
recommended by the U.N., the territory was awarded independence on July 1, 1960, when it then merged with the
former British Somaliland (over which the British had relinquished control a few days earlier) to form the independent Somali Republic (now Somali Democratic Republic). (See
Fig. 9.)

The U.N. decided the coastal region of Eritrea should
be federated with the Ethiopian state. The Federation of
Ethiopia and Eritrea, as it was sometimes called, became effective in 1952, with Eritrea retaining considerable internal
autonomy under the arrangement. However, the federation
was dissolved by the Ethiopian government in 1962, resulting
in the Eritrean area being totally annexed into the Ethiopian
state. Strong opposition by the Eritreans to that action
brought on a civil war that has since continued in Ethiopia.

IV.   NORTHWESTERN AFRICA

A.   Morocco

For many years, the sultanate of Morocco in north-western Africa had been divided into the protectorate of French Morocco, the protectorate of Spanish Morocco (with non-contiguous Northern and Southern Zones), the Spanish enclave of Ifni, and the diminutive international zone of Tangier (Fig. 20). France was first in terminating its pro-tectorate in the region, and French Morocco became the in-dependent Kingdom of Morocco on March 2, 1956. On April 17, the Spanish ended their protectorate over the Northern Zone of Spanish Morocco which then became part of the new kingdom. The Tangier Zone was also absorbed by the Mo-roccan state on October 29. Therefore, by the end of 1956, the core of the modern Moroccan state had been constituted.

Morocco would continue to grow by accretion. In 1958, the Spanish ceded the Southern Zone (Spanish Southern Mo-rocco) of their protectorate to Morocco, thereby extending the kingdom's effective territory to the northern boundary of Spanish Sahara. The Spanish also transferred the prov-ince of Ifni to Morocco in 1969. A few years later, Spain relinquished its claim to Spanish Sahara in a tripartite agree-ment signed with Morocco and Mauritania. Early in 1976, Morocco and Mauritania made final plans to partition the Spanish territory (by then generally known as Western Sa-hara), with the northern and central sections to be annexed by Morocco (Fig. 16).

When the Mauritanian government decided in 1979 to end its occupation of the southern portion of Western Sahara, Moroccan forces promptly moved into the area. The Moroccan government has since taken possession of the entire Western Sahara, but its claims to that region have been contested. (See Supp. Note IV-C for additional information on the dis-puted territory of Western Sahara.)

B.   Algeria and the Saharan Departments

Since the nineteenth century, Algeria had an excep-tional status among the French dependencies, and northern

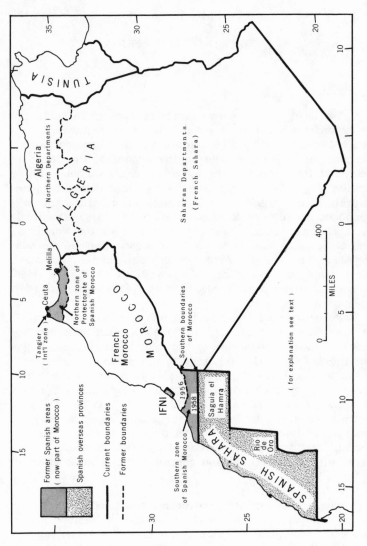

Fig. 20. Changes in the Political Map of Northwestern Africa.

Algeria was essentially integrated with the government of metropolitan France. By 1954, however, the worsening political climate ultimately brought an outbreak of open warfare between the Algerian nationalist forces and French troops. Hostilities continued until 1962 when Algeria was accorded status as an independent republic.

Although there was a centralized administration for the whole of French Algeria, the southern region of Algeria, comprising four military territories, had a different system of governance than that of the north. In 1957, the southern territories (Territoires du Sud) were by decree officially reconstituted as two Saharan Departments (Saoura and Oases). Furthermore, the new departments were assigned to the French Minister of State in Charge of Sahara and Overseas Territories. By these acts, southern Algeria, in effect being detached from the centralized administration in northern Algeria, was evolving into a discrete political entity (Fig. 20).

Establishing the Saharan Departments was the first stage of a comprehensive program for the economic and social development of France's Saharan possessions. In addition to southern Algeria, the proposed development area was to include portions of the Overseas Territories of Niger, Chad, and French Sudan (now Mali). The Common Organization for the Saharan Regions (Organisation Commune des Régions Sahariennes, or O.C.R.S.) was created in 1957 to direct the program. By 1959, however, O.C.R.S. was functioning only in the Saharan Departments of Saoura and Oases. Even the name French Sahara, intended for the extensive region once envisioned for O.C.R.S.'s activities, was being used only as a variant for southern Algeria.

The future status of the Saharan Departments, which the French sought to retain, was a major issue in the negotiations between Algerian and French leaders to end the war. The Algerians insisted that the Saharan Departments must be considered part of their national domain. The French finally acquiesced, relinquishing their claims to that area. Thus, when Algeria's independence was formally declared in July, 1962, the large southern region was integrated with northern Algeria to form the national territory.

C. Spanish Territories of the Western Saharan Region

During the 1930s, Spain sought to strengthen its control over certain territories in the Western Saharan region where its claims had been established by various treaties. Those territories included the colony of Río de Oro, the so-called "Occupied Zone" of Saguia el Hamra, and the small coastal enclave of Ifni (Fig. 20); the territory comprising Río de Oro and Saguia el Hamra was also generally called "Spanish Western Sahara," or, more simply, "Spanish Sahara." Until 1946, the territories remained integrated administratively with the Spanish Protectorate in Morocco. Spanish Sahara and Ifni were then reconstituted, by decree, as a new overseas entity called Spanish West Africa. Spanish Southern Morocco--technically the Southern Zone of the Spanish Protectorate--was attached for administrative convenience with Spanish Sahara, and generally considered part of Spanish West Africa.

(The whole of Spanish Sahara, it should be noted, was frequently referred to as Río de Oro, especially during the early part of this century. The name Río de Oro was often used for Spanish coastal possessions of the western Saharan region, even before boundaries had been delimited. Nevertheless, after the creation of Spanish Sahara in the mid-1930s, Río de Oro became the title used for one section of that larger unit. By 1946, Río de Oro was clearly established as the administrative district of the central and southern portions of Spanish Sahara [Fig. 20].)

Changes in the status of the component territories in 1958 resulted in the dissolution of Spanish West Africa. The Spanish government had ceded Southern Spanish Morocco to the Kingdom of Morocco, and the colonies of Ifni and Spanish Sahara were accorded official status as provinces of Spain. In 1969, the Spanish ceded Ifni to Morocco, leaving Spanish Sahara (or Province of Sahara) the sole Spanish possession along the western coast of Africa.

In 1975, the Spanish government finally decided to relinquish control of Spanish Sahara, by then informally, if not officially, known as "Western Sahara." The International Court of Justice supported the right of self-determination for the indigenous population of the territory. Disregarding that advisory opinion, Spain proceeded to conclude a tripartite

agreement with Mauritania and Morocco. The agreement provided for Spanish withdrawal at the end of 1975 and for the
territory to be divided between Morocco and Mauritania in
1976.

During 1975-76, the indigenous Saharan liberation
movement known as the Polisario Front (Popular Front for
the Liberation of Saguia el Hamra and Rio de Oro) declared
the partition illegal. The government-in-exile of the Polisario
Front, insistent on independence for Western Sahara, also
adopted Saharan Arab Democratic Republic (SADR) as the
official name for their homeland.

From 1976 to 1979, Morocco and Mauritania each administered a portion of Western Sahara (Fig. 16). By 1979,
the government of Mauritania, having reached a settlement
with the Polisario Front, decided to withdraw its control from
the southern areas. Moroccan forces thereupon entered the
southern region, completing a total annexation of the entire
Western Saharan territory. Moroccan claims to Western Sahara are being challenged, while the Polisario Front/SADR
has been receiving recognition and support from a number
of governments. Representatives of the SADR were even
admitted, overcoming considerable opposition, to the Organization of African Unity in 1982. As this was being written
in late 1986, Western Sahara was still a disputed territory,
and no settlement on its status had been reached.

V. FORMER BRITISH TERRITORIES OF
CENTRAL AND SOUTHERN AFRICA

A. Federation of Rhodesia and Nyasaland

The Federation of Rhodesia and Nyasaland, known
popularly as the Central African Federation, was constituted in October, 1953. The creation of the federation was
the realization of an oft-repeated suggestion to consolidate
the three British dependencies in Central Africa, viz., the
self-governing Crown Colony of Southern Rhodesia and the
protectorates of Northern Rhodesia and Nyasaland (Fig. 21).
Although a federal department was formed, each of the
three territories still kept its own administrative organization
with responsibility for internal affairs.

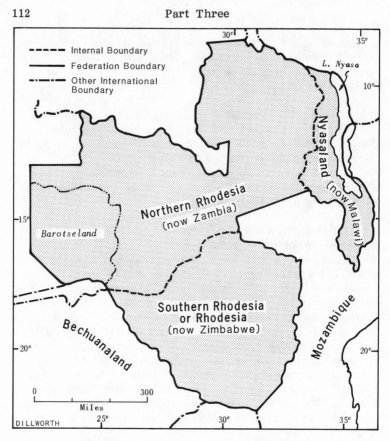

Fig. 21.   The Federation of Rhodesia
and Nyasaland, 1953-1963.

The federation was dissolved in December 1963. Re-
quests from Northern Rhodesia (now Zambia) and Nyasaland
(now Malawi) to withdraw from the federation had been approved even earlier by the British government; both were
given full independence in 1964. But the British government withheld granting independence to Southern Rhodesia,
then called simply Rhodesia. For reasons explained more
fully in Supp. Note V-B, Rhodesia would wait until 1980 to
receive formal recognition as a sovereign state.

B. Southern Rhodesia to Zimbabwe: The Prolonged Transition

Southern Rhodesia, at one time a territorial holding of

the British South Africa Company, was declared a self-
governing colony by the British government in 1923.   The
white settler minority was given considerable autonomy in
the internal administration of the colony.

In 1953, Southern Rhodesia was amalgamated with the
protectorates of Northern Rhodesia and Nyasaland in the
Federation of Rhodesia and Nyasaland (see Supp. Note V-A).
Following the federation's dissolution in 1963, Northern Rhodesia and Nyasaland were granted independence.   When
Northern Rhodesia became the Republic of Zambia in 1964,
the government of Southern Rhodesia announced the name of
its territory was being shortened to "Rhodesia"; subsequently, Rhodesia was generally used as the conventional name,
although the British Parliament never formally approved the
change.

The British government was withholding independence
until satisfied that the minority white government of Rhodesia
had made constitutional reforms providing for black majority
rule.   Unable to reach agreement with the British government
on this issue, the government of Rhodesia proclaimed its independence in November, 1965.   That unilateral declaration
of independence (UDI) was condemned as an illegal action:
Britain did not acknowledge Rhodesia's sovereignty, and no
other country or multinational association such as the U.N.
formally recognized the Rhodesian state.   As a consequence,
Rhodesia from 1965 to 1979 was to be a political territory
without status in the international community.   Outwardly
this appeared not to greatly concern the white leaders of
Rhodesia who even approved a new constitution in 1970 making the country a republic.

Yet by the early 1970s, confronted by mounting internal problems and international ostracism, the government of
Rhodesia finally initiated meetings with African political leaders.   After a few years, white minority and African leaders
agreed to form a multi-racial government dominated by black
Africans, though not in proportion to the actual number of
blacks in the total population.   A new constitution was promulgated in 1979, resulting in the establishment of a government for a country now to be called Zimbabwe Rhodesia.

Considerable dissatisfaction was expressed by many
groups, internally and externally, since the new political
structure left the white minority with considerable power.

Further conferences under British sponsorship were scheduled
between various factions in the country, and this led to the
dissolution of the parliament of Zimbabwe Rhodesia in December 1979. The territory, after fourteen years, reverted
briefly to British control (which, of course, had never been
relinquished legally). With the appointment of a British governor, the name Southern Rhodesia was also restored briefly
as the official name.

Following elections held in February 1980, a new government was organized. When the birth of the Republic of
Zimbabwe took place on April 18, 1980, its sovereign government received immediate formal recognition from Britain and
the community of world nations.

C. The High Commission Territories

The three British-administered dependencies of Basutoland, Bechuanaland Protectorate, and Swaziland in southern
Africa were known as the High Commission Territories (Fig.
22). Their status and administration were not comparable to
that of other British possessions. Although each territory
had a Resident Commissioner, general administrative responsibility for the three territories was vested in the High Commissioner of the United Kingdom resident in South Africa.

After the Union of South Africa was established in
1910, its leaders expected to eventually absorb the three
territories. Periodically, the South African government
urged Britain to terminate its special relationship with the
dependencies and to cede them to South Africa. However,
the South Africans' expectations were never fulfilled. African leaders in the Territories opposed plans which would
have incorporated their peoples into South Africa, even before World War II, but especially so after 1948 when the
South African government implemented apartheid and other
racially-discriminatory policies.

When South Africa terminated its membership in the
British Commonwealth in 1961, changes followed in Britain's
system of administering the High Commission Territories.
The office of High Commissioner was abolished in 1964, and
the government of each territory given greater internal
autonomy prior to achieving full independence. Bechuanaland

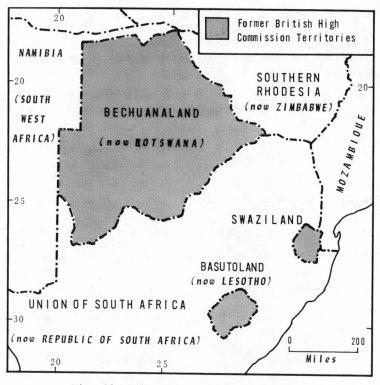

Fig. 22. The Former High Commission
Territories in Southern Africa.

became an independent republic in 1966, adopting the name
Botswana. In the same year, Basutoland became the Kingdom of Lesotho. With the granting of independence to the
Kingdom of Swaziland in 1968, three territories which once
might have been annexed by South Africa had all achieved
sovereign status.

VI. AFRICAN ISLANDS

A. Introduction

Because of the large number of national territories on

the African mainland, political events in the various islands associated with Africa, with the possible exception of Madagascar, might be overlooked. Yet the islands, onetime dependencies as were their mainland counterparts, also underwent changes in political status in recent decades (Table 2).

Table 2:

POLITICAL STATUS OF AFRICAN ISLANDS

Islands	Colonial Administration	Present Status and Name
Bioko	Portuguese	Independent. Part of the Republic of Equatorial Guinea.
Canary Islands*	-	-
Cape Verde Islands	Portuguese	Independent. Republic of Cape Verde.
Comoro Islands	French	Independent (except Mayotte). Federal Islamic Republic of the Comoros.
Madagascar	French	Independent. Democratic Republic of Madagascar.
Sao Tome and Principe	Portuguese	Independent. Democratic Republic of Sao Tome and Principe.
Zanzibar	British	Independent. Part of the United Republic of Tanzania.

*The Canary Islands are Spanish provinces and not considered colonies.

B. Zanzibar and Bioko: Islands United with Mainland Territories

A number of small offshore islands, usually with few or no inhabitants and having no economic significance, are included as parts of coastal African states. However, the offshore islands of Zanzibar and Bioko are noteworthy as each is a major division of a political state comprised of mainland and insular territories.

1. Zanzibar. The archipelago of Zanzibar, consisting primarily of the islands of Zanzibar and Pemba, is situated off the eastern coast of Africa (Fig. 9). The Sultan of Zanzibar's domain, including a narrow coastal strip on the mainland, was made a British protectorate in 1890. The coastal strip, known as the Kenya Protectorate, was linked for administrative purposes with Britain's Kenya Colony in the colonial period; for that reason, the total entity was officially designated the Kenya Colony and Protectorate. The Kenya Protectorate, ceded by the Sultan in December 1963, was then fully integrated into the new Kenya republic.

Zanzibar achieved full independence in December, 1963, but the new government was overthrown in early 1964, only a few weeks later. The long-form name, People's Republic of Zanzibar, was then adopted for the archipelago. Discussions between the governments of Zanzibar and Tanganyika culminated in an agreement (April 1964) to merge the two republics (into what now is known) as the United Republic of Tanzania. Nevertheless, the regional government of Zanzibar continues to exercise considerable authority in local matters. (For additional information on Tanzania, see Supp. Note I-D.)

2. Bioko (Fernando Po). The island of Bioko, for centuries known as Fernando Po (Poo), was later linked administratively by the Spanish with their mainland province of Rio Muni (Continental Spanish Guinea). From the late 1930s, the territories were referred to as the Spanish Territories of the Gulf of Guinea, and by the 1940s simply as Spanish Guinea. Later, the two colonies of Spanish Guinea were designated provinces within the collectivity of the Spanish Equatorial Region (1958–1963); in 1963 the provinces, joined in the entity renamed Equatorial Guinea, were given increased autonomy. The name Equatorial Guinea was retained for the political entity (mainland and islands) after Spanish rule ended in 1968 (Fig. 5).

During the 1970s, little information was available from or about the dictatorial regime in Equatorial Guinea. Standard sources found it difficult to provide authoritative accounts on internal developments, though occasionally there were announcements of places having been renamed, both in the mainland and insular divisions. With the approval of a new constitution in Equatorial Guinea in 1973, Fernando Po was renamed Macias Nguema Biyogo (variant: Macias Nguema Island). When the late president of the country, Francisco Macias Nguema Biyogo, fully Africanized his name to Masie Nguema Biyogo Negue Ndong, the island's name was also conveniently altered to Masie Nguema Biyogo!

The government was overthrown in 1979, and the new leadership began to make changes in place names. Among the most important was the renaming of the insular province, from Masie Nguema Biyogo to Bioko. (Nonetheless, some authorities still accept Fernando Po as an alternate name for the island.) Also, the smaller island of Annobon (Fig. 5), often administered with Bioko, became Pagalu in 1973, but reverted to its original name in the early 1980s.

C. Madagascar and the Comoro Islands

Madagascar, the largest of the islands usually associated with Africa, became a French colony in 1896. Later, the colony of the Comoro Islands was added as an administrative unit under the colonial government in Madagascar.

After France fell to the forces of Nazi Germany in 1940, Madagascar (including the Comoros) was under the control of the collaborationist Vichy regime. Commencing in May, 1942, however, British forces, offering strategic reasons as justification, undertook a takeover of Madagascar. The British agreed to an early transfer of political authority in Madagascar to the Free (Fighting) French, and that was completed by the beginning of 1943.

In 1946, Madagascar--like other French "colonies" of the pre-war period--was given status as an Overseas Territory of the Fourth French Republic. At that time, the Comoro Islands were administratively detached from Madagascar, also becoming a separate Overseas Territory.

When a new French constitution was presented in 1958
(see Supp. Note II-A), referenda were held in Madagascar
and the Comoros allowing the peoples of those territories
to decide if they desired to participate as members of the
French Community. The constitution was approved in both
areas: Madagascar elected to become an autonomous member-
state and was renamed Malagasy Republic, while the Comoros
opted to remain an Overseas Territory. The Malagasy Republic achieved full independence in 1960, though some years
later it would restore Madagascar (officially, the Democratic
Republic of Madagascar) as the name for the national state.

The Comoros continued under French rule until 1975
when officials on three of the four principal islands of the
archipelago announced a unilateral declaration of independence
(Fig. 7). Only on Mayotte island did the population reject
the proclamation of independence, preferring instead to continue under French administration. By the end of 1975,
therefore, the French had conceded the independence of the
three islands then comprising the Republic of the Comoros,
while claiming continuing authority in Mayotte. In referenda
held in 1974 and 1976, the population of Mayotte voted to
stay within the French Community.

The government of the Comoros has actively sought to
have Mayotte politically integrated with the other islands in
the Comoran state (renamed Federal Islamic Republic of the
Comoros in 1978), and its entreaties have been supported by
the United Nations. Such attempts at persuasion notwithstanding, the French have not abandoned Mayotte, giving it
special status as a "territorial collectivity."

D. Cape Verde Islands

The African Party for the Independence of Guinea-
Bissau and Cape Verde (Portuguese denomination: Partido
Africano da Independência da Guiné e Cabo Verde, or
PAIGC) was founded as a liberation movement which fought
to end Portuguese rule in Portuguese Guinea (now Guinea-
Bissau) on the mainland and in the Cape Verde Islands.
When each of the dependencies attained full independence,
PAIGC leaders assumed responsibility for organizing the new
governments. The party was considered binational, but each
political territory functioned as a sovereign state.

Total political unification of the republic of Guinea-Bissau and Cape Verde was seriously discussed for several years, though the merger was never consummated. Relations were severed between the two states in 1981. In Cape Verde a new political organization was created to replace PAIGC, thus bringing the binational party link to an end. Although diplomatic relations have since been restored between the two countries, unification appears unlikely.

VII. SECESSIONIST STATES

A. Introduction

Regional or ethnic organizations occasionally acquired sufficient strength to seriously threaten the internal unity of newly-independent African countries. There were numerous mutinies and rebel movements, causing chaos in specific locales and thereby contributing to the political instability in countries where new governments already were coping with organizational problems following decades of colonial rule. In retrospect, it is surprising that such movements rarely culminated in the actual secession of sub-territorial districts from the new national states. There were, however, two noteworthy examples of secessionist states: (1) Katanga (1960-1963), founded when a large southern province withdrew from Congo-Leopoldville (now Zaire); and (2) Biafra (1967-1970), devolved from the former Eastern Region of Nigeria. Both Katanga and Biafra survived as autonomous states for approximately thirty months, though not concurrently, and both also were ultimately reincorporated into the national states from which they had seceded.

B. Katanga

The large colony of the Belgian Congo became the independent Republic of the Congo (also known as Congo-Leopoldville) in June, 1960. The central government of the new state was confronted immediately with mutiny in the armed forces and by threats of secession from several regions. Only one secessionist state established relative autonomy for an extended period, that being the southern province of Katanga (Fig. 12).

When Katanga declared its independence in July, 1960, that action was repudiated by the Congolese government. Moreover, the Katangan government failed to receive formal recognition from any other country. A special United Nations force was organized to assist the central government in the military campaign against Katanga. In January, 1963, Katangan leaders agreed to end the secession, and the region was again joined to the national state.

By early 1963, a general reorganization of the internal divisions of Congo-Leopoldville had become effective. The six provinces inherited from the Belgian colonial regime were to be replaced by twenty-one new provinces; one result was the division of Katanga into three of the new provinces. Some years later, however, the government of Zaire (as the country is now known) decided to reduce the number of provinces. The Katanga region was reinstated as an internal division called Shaba Province.

C. Biafra

The British-administered Federation of Nigeria achieved independence in October 1960 and renamed Federal Republic of Nigeria in 1964. Although the federal administration had to deal with numerous problems in attempting to meet the needs of a large, diverse population, Nigeria for several years was regarded exemplary among the developing states of Africa. Nevertheless, internal differences intensified and by early 1967, the peoples of southeastern Nigeria--the Eastern Region, as then constituted--were demanding greater autonomy. Finding the federal government's responses unacceptable, the Eastern Region announced its withdrawal from the federal state on May 30, 1967, and the establishment of the Republic of Biafra was proclaimed (Fig. 2). The federal authorities condemned the secession as an illegal action taken by rebel leaders, and a period of civil war ensued.

The Nigerian civil war lasted thirty months. Unlike Katanga (see Supp. Note VII-B), which never received formal recognition from another national state, the government of Biafra was accorded such recognition by Gabon, Ivory Coast, Tanzania, and Zambia. The armed forces of the federal government eventually prevailed against the rebels, and the Biafran leaders surrendered in January 1970. The territory of the former Eastern Region was again incorporated into the Federal Republic of Nigeria.

In early 1967, prior to the secession of Biafra, the Nigerian government was proposing a reorganization of the country's primary internal divisions. Nigeria, which had been composed of four major regions and a federal district, was to be divided into twelve states. That proposal, calling for a division of the former Eastern Region into three of the new "state" units (Fig. 2), was implemented at the close of the civil war. (Nigeria was subsequently divided into nineteen states, causing further alternations in the pattern of internal divisions.)

VIII. THE "INDEPENDENT HOMELANDS" OF SOUTH AFRICA

Beginning in the late 1940s, the white-dominated government of South Africa issued a number of acts to implement its policy of "separate development" (e.g., Bantu Authorities Act of 1951, Bantu Self-Government Act of 1959, Bantu Homelands Constitution Act of 1971). Such legislation provided the legal basis for creating a number of semi-autonomous areas intended for exclusive occupation by black peoples. The special areas have been known by various names over the years--"Tribal Homelands," "Bantustans," "Bantu (or Black) Homelands," and now simply as "Homelands."

The South African government's long-range plan was to eventually grant full independence to each Homeland.   In October, 1976, the Republic of Transkei became the first of the Homelands to achieve independence (Fig. 23). That was followed, in succession, by (the Republics of) Bophuthatswana in December 1977, Venda in September 1979, and Ciskei in December 1981. In time, other Homelands were expected to join this group of "sovereign" states. [Independence for KwaNdebele, announced for late 1986, was apparently postponed.]

Both Transkei and Bophuthatswana comprise several non-contiguous areas (Fig. 23). The governments of those homeland states have expressed an understandable desire to

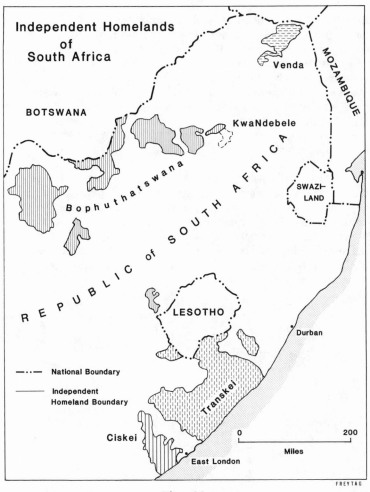

Fig. 23.

consolidate the fragmented units into viable political entities.
Such consolidation could be implemented either by an ex-
change of land or an outright acqusition of land from South
Africa. Several of the non-independent Homelands are similarly fragmented. Their leaders have been disinclined to discuss independence with the South African authorities until
the scattered units of their Homelands have been amalgamated.

      To date, the governments of the four "Independent

Homelands" have been recognized only by the parent Republic of South Africa. Furthermore, seats in the U.N. and the
Organization of African Unity (O.A.U.) have been denied representatives from those territories. Leaders of other African
countries and in the international community contend that the
nominally "Independent" Homelands are still dominated de facto
by South Africa. Critics have also observed that the program
for phased independence of the Homelands has been merely a
tactic to avoid bestowing full political rights on South Africa's
black population.

The South African government has recently indicated
that it might be reassessing the Homelands policies and perhaps be prepared to examine alternatives. For the present,
however, the four "independent Homelands" have no legal
standing internationally as sovereign states. They are,
therefore, only rarely shown on maps in other than South
African publications, and normally treated as quasi-autonomous
divisions of South Africa.

PART FOUR: SELECTED BIBLIOGRAPHY

This is a selected bibliography of published works which the author consulted regularly during the preparation of the gazetteer, maps, and supplementary notes.

BOOKS

The scope of each of the following books embraces the whole of Africa or one of the major regions. Books focusing on single countries have been purposely omitted. Admittedly, a book title here and there might appear to suggest concentration on one country, though the contents will be found actually to cover a larger region covering several political states.

Abshire, David M., and Samuels, Michael A., eds. Portuguese Africa: A Handbook. New York: Praeger, 1969.

Africa. Oxford Regional Economic Atlas. London: Oxford University Press, 1965.

Akintoye, S. A. Emergent African States: Topics in Twentieth Century African History. London: Longman Group, 1976.

Alexander, Lewis. World Political Patterns. 2nd ed. Chicago: Rand McNally, 1963. Chaps. 14, 15, 16.

Alman, Mirian, ed. Debates of African Legislatures. Standing Conference on Library Materials on Africa (SCOLMA). Cambridge, Eng.: Heffer, 1972.

Barbour, Nevill, ed. A Survey of North West Africa (The
    Maghrib). 2nd ed. London: Oxford University Press,
    1962.

Becker, George Henry, Jr. The Disposition of the Italian
    Colonies 1941-1951. Université de Genève, Institut
    Universitaire de Hautes Études Internationales. Anne-
    masse: Imprimerie Granchamp, 1952.

Best, Alan C. G., and de Blij, H. African Survey. New
    York: Wiley, 1977.

Boateng, E. A. A Political Geography of Africa. Cambridge,
    Eng.: Cambridge University Press, 1978.

Bowman, Isaiah. The New World: Problems in Political
    Geography. 4th ed. Yonkers-on-Hudson, N.Y.: World
    Book, 1928. Chap. 33.

Brelsford, W. V., ed. Handbook to the Federation of Rho-
    desia and Nyasaland. London: Cassell, 1960.

The Cambridge History of Africa. Vol. 8. From c. 1940 to
    c. 1975. Cambridge, Eng.: Cambridge University Press,
    1984.

Carter, Gwendolen M., ed. Five African States: Responses
    to Diversity. Ithaca, N.Y.: Cornell University Press,
    1963.

_____, ed. Politics in Africa: 7 Cases. New York:
    Harcourt, Brace & World, 1966.

Catchpole, Brian, and Akinjogbin, I. A. A History of West
    Africa in Maps and Diagrams. London: Collins Educa-
    tional, 1984.

Christopher, A. J. Colonial Africa. Totowa, N.J.: Barnes
    & Noble, 1984.

Church, R. J. Harrison, West Africa. 8th ed. New York:
    Longman, 1981.

_____. West Africa: Environment and Policies. 2nd ed.
    New York: Van Nostrand, 1976.

Cohen, Robin, ed. African Islands and Enclaves. Beverly Hills, Calif.: Sage Publications, 1983.

Davis, N. E. A History of Southern Africa. 2nd ed. New York: Longman, 1978.

Day, Alan J., ed. Border and Territorial Disputes. A Keesing's Reference Publication. Detroit: Gale, 1982.

Dore, Isaak I. The International Mandate System and Namibia. Boulder, Colo.: Westview Press, 1985.

Drysdale, Alasdair, and Blake, Gerald H. The Middle East and North Africa: A Political Geography. New York: Oxford University Press, 1985.

Duignan, Peter, and Gann, L. H. Colonialism in Africa, 1870-1960. Vol. 5. A Bibliographical Guide to Colonialism in Sub-Saharan Africa. London: Cambridge University Press, 1973.

East, W. G., and Moodie, A. E., eds. The Changing World: Studies in Political Geography. Yonkers, N.Y.: World Book Co., 1956. Chaps. XXX, XXXI, XXXIII.

Fage, J. D. An Atlas of African History. 2nd revised ed. New York: Holmes & Meier, 1978.

_____. A History of Africa. New York: Knopf, 1978. Part 4.

Fitzgerald, Walter. Africa: A Social, Economic and Political Geography of Its Major Regions. 3rd ed. New York: Dutton, 1939.

Freeman-Grenville, G. S. P. A Modern Atlas of African History. London: Rex Collins, 1976.

Gailey, Harry A., Jr. History of Africa from 1800 to Present. New York: Holt, Rinehart, and Winston, 1972.

Gann, Lewis H. Central Africa: The Former British States. Englewood Cliffs, N.J.: Prentice-Hall, 1971.

Gorman, Robert F. Political Conflict on the Horn of Africa. New York: Praeger, 1981.

Great Britain. Naval Intelligence Division. French Equatorial
Africa and Cameroons. Geographical Handbook Series.
H.M.S.O. [Oxford: Oxford University Press], 1942.

_____. French West Africa. Vol. I. The Federation.
Vol. II. The Colonies. Geographical Handbook Series.
H.M.S.O. [Oxford: Oxford University Press], 1944.

Griffiths, Ieuan Ll. An Atlas of African Affairs. London:
Methuen, 1984.

Hailey, William Malcolm [Lord Hailey]. An African Survey:
A Study of Problems Arising in Africa South of the Sahara. 2nd ed. New York: Oxford University Press,
1945.

_____. An African Survey, Revised 1956: A Study of
Problems Arising in Africa South of the Sahara. London:
Oxford University Press, 1957.

_____. The Republic of South Africa and the High Com-
mission Territories. London: Oxford University Press,
1963.

Hallett, Robin. Africa Since 1875: A Modern History. Ann
Arbor: University of Michigan Press, 1974.

Hance, William A. The Geography of Modern Africa. 2nd
ed. New York: Columbia University Press, 1975.

Historical Atlas of Africa. Edited by J. F. Ade Ajayi and
Michael Crowder. New York: Cambridge University
Press, 1985.

Hodges, Tony. Western Sahara: The Roots of a Desert
War. Westport, Conn.: Lawrence Hill, 1983.

Hodgson, Robert D., and Stoneman, E. A. The Changing
Map of Africa. 2nd ed. Princeton, N.J.: Van Nostrand,
1968.

Kimble, George H. T. Tropical Africa. Vol. 2. Society
and Polity. New York: The Twentieth Century Fund,
1960.

Kirchherr, Eugene C. Abyssinia to Zimbabwe: A Guide to the Political Units of Africa in the Period 1947-1978. 3rd ed. Africa Series No. 25. Athens: Ohio University Press, 1979.

Legum, Colin, and Lee, Bill. Conflict in the Horn of Africa. New York: Africana Publishing, 1978.

Long, David E., and Reich, Bernard, eds. The Government and Politics of the Middle East and North Africa. Boulder, Colo.: Westview Press, 1980.

Maisel, Albert Q. Africa: Facts and Forecasts. New York: Duell, Sloan and Pearce, 1943.

Malan, T., and Hattingh, P.S. Black Homelands in South Africa. Pretoria: African Institute of South Africa, 1976.

McEwan, P. J. M., ed. Twentieth-Century Africa. London: Oxford University Press, 1968.

McEwen, A. C. International Boundaries of East Africa. London: Oxford University Press, 1971.

Moon, Parker Thomas. Imperialism and World Politics. New York: Macmillan, 1926.

Mortimore, Edward. France and the Africans, 1944-1960. New York: Walker, 1969.

Oliver, Roland, and Atmore, Anthony. Africa Since 1800. 3rd ed. New York: Cambridge University Press, 1981.

Prothero, R. Mansell, ed. A Geography of Africa: Regional Essays on Fundamental Characteristics, Issues, and Problems. New York: Praeger, 1969.

Rennell, Francis J. [Lord Rennell of Rodd]. British Military Administration of Occupied Territories in Africa During the Years 1941-1947. London: His Majesty's Stationery Office, 1948.

Rivlin, Benjamin. The United Nations and the Italian Colonies. New York: Carnegie Endowment for International Peace, 1950.

Sagay, J. O., and Wilson, D. A. Africa: A Modern History (1800-1975). New York: Holmes & Meier, 1979.

Stevens, Richard P. Lesotho, Botswana, and Swaziland: The Former High Commission Territories in Southern Africa. New York: Praeger, 1967.

Stillman, Calvin W., ed. Africa in the Modern World. Chicago: University of Chicago Press, 1955.

Thompson, Virginia, and Adolff, Richard. The Emerging States of French Equatorial Africa. Stanford, Calif.: Stanford University Press, 1960.

_____, and _____. French West Africa. Stanford, Calif.: Stanford University Press, 1957.

Touval, Saadia. The Boundary Politics of Independent Africa. Cambridge, Mass.: Harvard University Press, 1972.

U.S. Department of State. Bureau of Intelligence and Research. The Geographer. Africa: Pattern of Sovereignty. Geographic Bulletin No. 6, revised. Washington, D.C.: GPO, 1968.

_____, _____. The Geographer. Survey of the French Republic. Geographic Bulletin No. 4. Washington, D.C.: GPO, 1965.

_____. The Geographer. Portugal and Overseas Provinces. Geographic Report No. 5. [Washington, D.C.: GPO, 1961.]

Wallbank, T. Walter. Contemporary Africa: Continent in Transition. Revised ed. Princeton, N.J.: Van Nostrand, 1964.

Ward, W. F., and White, L. W. East Africa: A Century of Change, 1870-1970. New York: Africana Publishing, 1971.

Wells, Carvath. Introducing Africa. New York: Putnam, 1944.

White, Dorothy Shipley. Black Africa and De Gaulle: From
the French Empire to Independence. University Park:
Pennsylvania State University Press, 1979.

Widstrand, Carl Gosta, ed. African Boundary Problems.
Uppsala, Sweden: The Scandinavian Institute of African
Studies, 1969.

Wilson, Henry S. The Imperial Experience in Sub-Saharan
Africa Since 1870. Minneapolis: University of Minnesota
Press, 1977.

Wohlgemuth, Patricia. "The Portuguese Territories and the
United Nations." International Conciliation, No. 545
(November 1963).

Zartman, I. William. Government and Politics in Northern
Africa. New York: Praeger, 1963.

PERIODICALS, YEARBOOKS, AND GENERAL
REFERENCE WORKS

Africa Contemporary Record: Annual Survey and Documents.
Edited by Colin Legum. New York: Africana Publishing.
Published annually.

Africa Independent: A Survey of Political Developments.
Keesing's Research Report. New York: Scribner, 1972.

Africa Report. Published bimonthly by the African-American
Institute. New Brunswick, N.J.: Transactions Periodi-
cals Consortium, Rutgers University. (Formerly Africa
Special Report [1956-1960].)

Africa South of the Sahara. London: Europa Publications.
Published annually.

African Research Bulletin: Political, Social, and Cultural
Series. London: Africa Research. Published monthly.

Americana Annual: Yearbook of the Encyclopedia Americana.
Danbury, Conn.: Grolier Enterprises, Inc.

The Annual Register: A Record of World Events. Harlow,
    Essex, U.K.: Longman. Published annually.

Britannica Book of the Year. Chicago: Encyclopaedia
    Britannica, Inc. Published annually.

Brownlie, Ian. African Boundaries: A Legal and Diplomatic
    Encyclopaedia. Berkeley: University of California Press,
    1979.

The Cambridge Encyclopedia of Africa. Edited by Roland
    Oliver and Michael Crowder. Cambridge, England: Cam-
    bridge University Press, 1981.

Cartactual. Budapest, Hungary: Geocartographic Research
    Dept., Institute of Geodesy and Cartography. Bimonthly
    map service.

Cook, Chris, and Killingray, David. African Political Facts
    Since 1945. New York: Facts on File, 1983.

Daggs, Elisa. All Africa: All Its Political Entites of Inde-
    pendent or Other Status. New York: Hastings House,
    1970.

Facts on File: World News Digest with Index. New York:
    Facts on File. Published weekly.

Freeman-Grenville, G. S. P. Chronology of African History.
    London: Oxford University Press, 1973.

Geographical Digest. London: Philip. Published annually.

Keesing's Contemporary Archives: Record of World Events.
    Harlow, Essex, U.K.: Longman. Published weekly until
    1983; now published monthly.

Kitchen, Helen, ed. A Handbook of African Affairs. New
    York: Praeger, 1964.

League of Nations. Economic Intelligence Service. Statisti-
    cal Year-Book of the League of Nations. Geneva [Switzer-
    land: League of Nations]. Published annually until World
    War II.

Legum, Colin, ed. Africa Handbook. Revised edition.
Harmondsworth, Middlesex, Eng.: Penguin, 1969.

The Middle East and North Africa. London: Europa.
Published annually.

The New York Times. New York: New York Times.
Published daily.

Phillips, Claude S. The African Political Dictionary. Santa
Barbara, Calif.: ABC-Clio Information Services, 1984.

Political Handbook of the World. Binghampton, N.Y.: CSA
Publications, 1986. Published every 2-3 years.

Rosenthal, Eric. Encyclopedia of Southern Africa. 6th ed.
London: Warne, 1973.

Shimoni, Yaacov, and Levine, Evytar, eds. Political Dictionary of the Middle East in the 20th Century. Revised edition. New York: Quadrangle, 1974.

Standard Encyclopaedia of Southern Africa. 12 vols. Cape
Town [South Africa]: NASOU Limited, 1970.

The Statesman's Year-Book. New York: St. Martin's.

Taylor, Sidney, ed. The New Africans: A Guide to the
Contemporary History of Emergent Africa and Its Leaders.
(Reuters Guide.) New York: Putnam, 1967.

UN Chronicle. New York: United Nations Office of Public
Information. Published monthly, except August. (Suc-
cessor to United Nations Bulletin [1946-1954], United Nations Review [1954-1964], and UN Monthly Chronicle
[1964-1975]).

Wattenberg, Ben, and Smith, Ralph Lee. The New Nations
of Africa. New York: Hart, 1963.

West Africa. London: West Africa Publishing Co. Published
weekly.

GAZETTEERS AND OTHER SOURCES ON
GEOGRAPHICAL NAMES

Barnhart, Clarence L., and Halsey, William D., eds. The New Century Cyclopedia of Names. 3 vols. New York: Appleton-Century-Crofts, 1954.

The Columbia-Lippincott Gazetteer of the World, with 1961 Supplement. Edited by Leon E. Seltzer. New York: Columbia University Press, 1962.

International Federation of Library Associations and Institutions. International Office of UBC [Universal Bibliographic Control]. Names of States: An Authority List of Language Forms for Catalogue Entries / Compiled by the IFLA International Office for UBC. London: IFLA International Office for UBC, 1981.

The International Geographic Encyclopedia and Atlas. Boston: Houghton Mifflin, 1979.

Lana, Gabriella; Iasbez, Liliana; and Meak, Lidia, comps. Glossary of Geographical Names in Six Languages. New York: American Elsevier, 1967.

The Macmillan World Gazetteer and Geographical Dictionary. Edited by T. C. Collocott and J. O. Thorne. New York: Macmillan, 1955.

United Nations. Food and Agriculture Organization. Names of Countries and Their Capital Cities including Adjectives of Nationality and Currency Units. Terminology Bulletin, no. 20, rev. 7, 1984.

U.S. Board on Geographic Names. Foreign Name Decisions of the U.S. Board on Geographic Names. Washington: Defense Mapping Agency. Issued irregularly.

U.S. Defense Mapping Agency. Gazetteer of Conventional Names. Names Approved by the United States Board on Geographic Names. 2nd ed. Washington: 1977.

U.S. Defense Mapping Agency Topographic Center. Africa and Southwest Asia. Official Standard Names Approved

by the U.S. Board on Geographic Names. Gazetteer
Supplement, 1972.

U.S. Department of State. Bureau of Intelligence and Research. Status of the World's Nations. Dept. of State
Publication 8735. Revised and reissued on irregular
basis.

U.S. Department of State. Bureau of Intelligence and Research. The Geographer. Geographic Notes. Issued
irregularly.

U.S. Department of the Interior. Board on Geographic
Names. Decisions on Miscellaneous Foreign Names.
Decision List No. 5303. June, 1953.

U.S. Geographic Board. First Report on Foreign Geographic
Names. Washington: U.S. Government Printing Office,
1932.

Webster's Geographical Dictionary. Springfield, Mass.:
Merriam. Editions of 1949 and 1967.

Webster's New Geographical Dictionary. Springfield, Mass.:
Merriam. Editions of 1972, 1980, and 1984.

Wilcocks, Julie. Countries and Islands of the World: A
Guide to Nomenclature. London: Bingley, 1981.

SPECIAL SOURCES

African Historical Dictionaries.

Series of special reference books; each volume prepared by a specialist for one country. Published irregularly
by Scarecrow Press, Metuchen, N.J. Series includes volumes
for about forty African countries.

Area Handbook Series (Country Studies).

Each volume produced by an interdisciplinary team of

specialists and focused on a specific country. Prepared by
Foreign Area Studies of The American University, Washington, D.C., with volumes issued irregularly by the U.S.
Government Printing Office. At one time, each volume appeared under the title, Area Handbook of [name of country];
now each is issued with the title [name of country]:   A
Country Study.

Area Handbooks (Country Studies) are available for
more than thirty African countries, several already in second
and third editions.

International Boundary Studies.

Special reports, each on a specific international boundary (technically, a boundary segment), including a detailed
description of the course of the boundary with historical
notes. Studies issued irregularly by the Office of Geographer, U.S. Department of State. Series provides extensive
coverage for international boundaries in Africa.